Supremely Good

And Other Foundational Texts of the Bible

Doug Hallman

authorHOUSE

AuthorHouse™
1663 Liberty Drive
Bloomington, IN 47403
www.authorhouse.com
Phone: 833-262-8899

Published by AuthorHouse 04/13/2021

ISBN: 978-1-6655-1774-4 (sc)
ISBN: 978-1-6655-1775-1 (e)

Contents

Chapter 1   Supremely Good 1

Chapter 2   Emmanuel 11

Chapter 3   All Things Good 20

Chapter 4   I Hear You 29

Chapter 5   If My People 37

Chapter 6   My Shepherd 51

Chapter 7   What God Wants 66

Chapter 8   Every Sin Forgiven 71

Chapter 9   When You Pray..85

Chapter 10 A Great Paradox.....................................97

Chapter 11 God Loves 112

Chapter 12 They Will Kill Him.............................. 125

Chapter 13 Raised from the Dead........................... 136

Chapter 14 A Three-Ply Cord 145

Index of Scripture References 159

Acknowledgments

This book is drawn from lessons presented to the BYKOTA (Be Ye Kind One To Another) Sunday School Class at the First United Methodist Church in Lakeland, Florida. My appreciation is extended to the faithful members of the class for their feedback and encouragement to bring these chapters to print.

To RayaSue, my loving wife. I owe more than can be said for her patience during this process, and for her amazing and thorough proofreading and editing skills.

And to Robert Weatherall, friend and colleague, who has encouraged, prodded, and nudged me for many years to write this book.

Preface

Foundational Texts of the Bible

The earliest memory I have about the Bible is the story of David and the giant. I remember it because of the mighty slingshot David used to kill the giant. (I could never remember the giant's name until much later.) One stone, and *blam*—the giant was dead. I think that made such an impression on me because on an early vacation, Mom and Dad had let my brother and me buy slingshots at an "Indian trading post" in Cherokee, North Carolina. We had practiced picking up small rocks by the river and aiming at trees. After many tries, I was finally able to get the rock to stay in the little leather pouch long enough for me to pull back on the rubber band and let 'er fly! It was quite a bit later that I was able to send it flying far enough to resemble anything like an actual shot.

The reason I remember all of that is because the Bible told me that with a slingshot, a little kid like me could defend himself against the giants of the world, or at least against the big kids in the neighborhood. I finally realized, however, that at least in my hands, a slingshot was no deadly weapon.

I learned the story of David and Goliath in Sunday school, where I could be found each and every Sunday morning at 9:45. In our house, the question was never, "Are we going to church today?" Rather, it was, "What time are we leaving?" As a result of all those hours in Sunday school, I picked up knowledge of a whole lot of Bible stories: Samson and his haircut. (I thought about that every month while sitting in Sid the barber's chair. Sid always gave us a piece of bubble gum if we sat still. That was the only gum I ever got in those days, and I wondered if Samson got the same reward when he got his haircut. It was also the only time I got to read comic books!) I remember hearing about the guy who fell overboard and got swallowed by the whale. (That image would haunt me whenever we went fishing in my dad's boat.) Then there was Moses parting the sea. (C. B. Demille let me know just how that scene looked.) At Christmas each year, we built the barn for our nativity scene out of Lincoln Logs (it was the fifties after all). Each year, there was a debate over just how the barn was built last year because it somehow seemed important to build it exactly like the original barn that Jesus was born in.

There were so many stories and scenes from the Bible that I learned about in those early years that by the time I reached junior high school, I thought I pretty much knew the Bible! As the years went on and I kept going to youth group and church camp, I picked up more and more knowledge about the Bible. However, if you had asked me the direct question, "What is the Bible all about?" I would have likely given the answer that so many kids over the years gave me when I asked them. I would have paused and then said, "God."

Over the past five decades while serving as pastor of local churches, I have become aware that most people have pretty much the same level of biblical knowledge that I had early on. They know there are a lot of interesting stories, there are some memorable characters, the stories about Jesus are in there somewhere, and it gets really scary at the end!

Most people know that the Bible is really a compilation of a number of books. Some people can even name a few of the books. However, while teaching the Bible at the college level, I was amused (and startled) by the lack of any real understanding many college students from privileged homes and families had about the Bible. Among the names of Bible books I read about in term papers were Geniuses, Palms, Collipians, and Philoppians. Many of those students had no idea what the Old and New Testaments were. One kid asked me if Moses and Jesus were brothers!

In more recent years, I have been disturbed and disheartened by the way so many people go to the Bible to prove their point on a subject by selecting one verse that sounds like it addresses the issue. I could give pages of examples of what I am talking about, but I think this one is enough to make my point. A racist church member essentially told me, though in slightly different words,

"God is white and doesn't like Black people because the Bible says in 1 John 1:5 that 'God is light and in him is no darkness at all.'" Wow!

Then there are the folks (often new Christians) who make the pledge to read the whole Bible, cover to cover, as though it were a novel. That is a noble goal, but I sense that a lot of those pledge takers lose some of that enthusiasm when they get to Numbers and all those "begets," or some of the obscure historical references in the prophets. The problem is the Bible is not a novel, and though I am suggesting that there is a single theme threaded throughout, there are a whole lot of stories that don't seem to be connected at first glance.

But the Bible is more than just sixty-six separate books, and there is more to it than just a bunch of interesting stories. There is a point, a message, from start through to the end. That unified message builds and grows but remains the same from the Old Testament through the New Testament. That message is like the three-stranded cord mentioned in Ecclesiastes 4:12—it is stronger when woven together than when taken apart. When we begin to think about what is the consistent message of the Bible that threads through all its pages, the Bible becomes a much stronger foundation for our faith than if all we know about it is a few of its stories.

In this book, I hope to draw out some of the threads of that message and braid them together into a stronger cord of understanding than the reader might otherwise have thought about. I will do that by identifying some of what I am calling the "Foundational Texts" of the Bible and following those strands of thought as they are repeated and threaded throughout the Bible. The Bible is more than a collection of stories. The Bible is *the* story about the eternal God's relationship with us faulty humans, the beloved children of God. It is one message from Genesis through to Revelation—and it is a good one!

Chapter 1

Supremely Good

God saw everything he had made: it was supremely good.
—Genesis 1:31

WHAT IS SUPREMELY GOOD? THIS world is. It's all good—very good. Every part of it is good. More than good. Great, even! Supremely good

Just to be sure, I looked up the simple word *good* in the dictionary. (Yes, I still have one, and I know how to use it—sorry, Google.) What I found were almost thirty little subheadings giving various ways we use the word. In fact, in my *American Heritage New College Dictionary*, the listing for *good* takes up a full quarter of a page, all of it ending with the note that it is derived from the Middle English *gode*. From the appendix on word origins in that dictionary is the note that *good* is traced back to the German root *ghedh*, meaning "to unite; to join; to fit."

Something is good when it all fits together—when all the parts join forces for the purpose for which it was

1

created. The Bible is built on a foundation that includes the statement that God looked at the creation and said, "It is supremely good."

In fact, the name we use for the Divine Creator, God, comes directly from the word *good*.

> As Jesus continued down the road, a man ran up, knelt before him, and asked, "Good Teacher, what must I do to obtain eternal life?" Jesus replied, "Why do you call me good? No one is good except God alone." (Mark 10:17–18)

I suggest that the verse "God saw everything he made and it was supremely good" is foundational to the message of the entire Bible because of the affirmation it makes about the creation—and not just parts of the creation like the mountains of North Carolina, but the whole thing. It is *all* good. It's the beautiful stage on which the great drama of life is performed!

If I were to ask a group of people to list the good and bad types of weather or geological events, I'm sure the list of good things would include rain, but not too much at one time; snow, but not too much at one time; sunshine; and cool breezes on a summer day. I'm not sure any meteorological or geological events such as hurricanes, tornadoes, earthquakes, volcanic eruptions, hailstorms, lightning storms, subfreezing temperatures, or floods would make the good list.

We categorize things as good or bad by how they affect us. To me, cooked broccoli is not good. Deep snow is (I'm from Miami). You might think otherwise. You would likely have a hard time finding anyone in New Orleans or Puerto Rico who would say a good thing about hurricanes. Or anyone along the Mississippi River who would be thankful for floods. Or folks in the Midwest who would praise tornadoes. Okay, maybe a couple, but you get my point.

But these are all parts of the creation that God looked at and said, "This is supremely good!" If that statement is not true, then we live in a dangerous world that cannot be trusted, and the rest of the Bible is left shrouded in a dark cloud of fear. However, it is the truth of that statement that distinguishes the Judeo-Christian faith from most of the other religious expressions of the ancient world. And that is what makes it foundational.

Not every religion is based on the foundation that "everything is supremely good." Imagine living with a worldview of creation in which all that is in the world is not supremely good. Imagine waking up every morning believing something like the Mesopotamian creation myth, the *Enuma Elish*.

> Life began after an epic battle between the elder gods and the younger. In the beginning there was only water swirling in chaos, and nothing separated the fresh from the bitter. These waters represented two distinct principles: the male principle, named Apsu, was the fresh water; the female principle, Tiamat, was salt water. From the union of these two principles, all the other gods came into being.

Those younger gods were so loud in their daily arguing with each other that they began to annoy the elder gods, especially Apsu; so he decided to kill them all. Tiamat, however, was shocked at Apsu's plot and warned one of her sons, Ea, the god of wisdom and intelligence. With the help of his brothers and sisters, Ea put Apsu to sleep and then killed him. Out of the corpse of Apsu, Ea created the earth and built his home.

Stay with me …

Tiamat, upset now over Apsu's death, raised the forces of chaos to destroy her children herself. Ea and his siblings fought against their mother, Tiamat, and her allies without success until from among them rose the great storm god, Marduk. Marduk swore he would defeat Tiamat if the gods would proclaim him their king. This agreed to, he entered into battle with Tiamat and killed her. From her upper body he created the sky, and from the lower parts of her body he formed the earth. He then continued with the act of creation to make human beings from the drippings of her blood. Humans were formed to be nothing more than servants of the gods! (Enuma Elish - The Babylonian Epic of Creation; Article by Joshua J. Markby; May, 4, 2018)

Or perhaps you would prefer the view of creation from China, during the period of the Middle Kingdom.

A cosmic egg floated within the timeless void, containing the opposing forces of yin and yang. After eons of incubation, the first being, Pan-gu, emerged. The heavy parts (yin) of the egg drifted downwards, forming the earth. The lighter parts (yang) rose to form the sky. Pan-gu, fearing the parts might re-form, stood upon the earth and held up the sky. He grew ten feet per day for 18,000 years, until the sky was 30,000 miles high. His work completed, he died.

His parts transformed into elements of the universe—animals, weather phenomena, and celestial bodies. Some say the fleas on him became humans. Another explanation for the origin of humans is that the goddess Nuwa was lonely so she fashioned men out of mud from the Yellow River. Those first humans delighted her, but took too long to make, so she flung muddy droplets over the earth, each one becoming a new person. These hastily made people became the commoners, while the earlier ones became the nobles. (Chinese Origin Story: Pan Gu and the Egg of the World; Kahn Academy.org; Compiled by Cynthia Stokes Brown

Not fond of that one either? The ancient Egyptians had several creation myths. All begin with the swirling, chaotic waters of Nu (or Nun).

> Atum willed himself into being and then created a hill to stand on. Atum was genderless and possessed an all-seeing eye. He/She spat out a son, Shu, god of the air. Atum then vomited up a daughter, Tefnut, goddess of moisture. These two were charged with the task of creating order out of chaos. Shu and Tefnut generated Geb, the earth, and Nut, the sky. First the earth and sky were entwined, but then Geb lifted Nut above him. Gradually the world's order formed, but Shu and Tefnut became lost in the remaining darkness. Atum removed her/his all-seeing eye and sent it in search of them. When Shu and Tefnut returned, thanks to the eye, Atum wept with joy. Presumably he/she had reinserted the eye at that point because where her/his tears struck the earth, humans sprang up. (Ra, The Creator God of Ancient Egypt; By Fayza Haikal; The American University in Cairo

How would you like to go to Sunday school and be taught something like that? How would you like to live believing that you were created out of parts of a dead god, or out of mud thrown around by a frustrated god, or out of the tears of a cyclops?

What makes the creation good according to our faith

is that God, who is eternal and had no reason to create anything, chose to create a beautiful world in which everything is good. God then chose to create humanity in God's own image and to gift us with all the beauty and goodness of creation because of his love toward us. (We are, after all, his favorites!)

The earth is not made from the corpse of a defeated god. We are not formed of the dripping blood of a slain god. We were not created from the teardrops of a cyclops. We were, we thankfully believe, created by the God who had no reason to create at all other than the fact that God is love and love has to be expressed. (According to Oscar Hammerstein III, "Love isn't love until it is given away.") We are given authority over all the earth and were not created simply to be the servants of violent, capricious gods.

We may get caught in the winds of a hurricane, the wildfires of a dry forest, or the tremors of an earthquake, but that doesn't make those things "bad." They are, each one, good. They are all part of the machinery of this dynamic creation, and each part is required to keep the whole thing functioning.

Volcanoes release heat that builds up beneath the earth's crust. Volcanoes provide nutrients to the surrounding soil. Volcanic ash contains minerals that are beneficial to plants as it mixes with the soil. Volcanic gases are the source of all the water and most of the atmosphere that we have today. (I don't understand that, but I read it in a very reliable source.) Volcanos make islands and add to the continents.

Earthquakes provide a picture of what's going on underground, which can make oil and gas extraction more efficient and allow scientists to monitor the progress of water during geothermal energy extraction.

Droughts give the land a rest from production. Floods replenish nutrients in the soil far from the banks of rivers.

Lightning strikes help dissolve unusable nitrogen in water, which then creates a natural fertilizer that plants can absorb through their roots. Lightning also produces ozone, a vital gas in our atmosphere that helps shield the planet from rays of harmful ultraviolet sunlight (and a gas that we have become rather efficient at depleting).

Hurricanes are efficient drought busters. They break up red tide. They provide a global heat balance. They replenish barrier islands and inland plant life.

The creation is a system, and the thing that makes it good is that all the parts work together. The creation is good because it services the purpose for which it came into being: the sustaining of life! The creation is unified, it fits, and it functions together as a unit. The fact that we continue to live on the slopes of volcanos or on barrier islands or in tornado alleys and suffer the consequences of those areas says more about our stubbornness than about God's anger.

That declaration in Genesis that the creation and all of its parts is supremely good is foundational to our belief in and willingness to obey the laws of the God of creation. If we did not believe that the creation and all its parts is good, if we had any doubts about the goodness of God, and if we were left to wonder if a destructive tornado was the vengeful act of an angry God, we might be unwilling to risk our lives, love our enemies, or sacrifice to do good to those who harm us. We might question why it is necessary to spend time or energy helping those in need who have nothing to give us in return.

The bottom line, the foundational principle of our faith, is that we believe in a God who is always only good. We see that in the creation, and in that goodness is our peace and our lives!

O Lord, our Lord, how majestic is
your name in all the earth!
You made your glory higher than heaven!

From the mouths of nursing babies you
have laid a strong foundation
because of your foes, in order to stop vengeful enemies.

When I look up at your skies, at
what your fingers made—
the moon and the stars that you set firmly in place—
what are human beings that you think about us;
what are human beings that you pay attention to us?
You've made us only slightly less than divine,
crowning us with glory and grandeur.

You've let us rule over your handiwork,
putting everything under our feet—

all sheep and all cattle, the wild animals too,
the birds in the sky, the fish in the ocean,
everything that travels the pathways of the sea.

O Lord, our Lord, how majestic is your
name in all the earth! (Psalm 8)

Chapter 2

Emmanuel

You will call him Emmanuel which means "God with us."
—Matthew 1:23

HERE'S A QUESTION FOR YOU: When God threw Adam and Eve out of the garden and locked the gate, where was God? Tick-tock ... tick-tock ... tick-tock ... Time's up!

If you tried looking up the exact answer to my question in Genesis, you did not find it. The answer is not found in one verse. The answer to the question "Where was God after God tossed Adam and Eve out of the garden?" is that God was outside the garden with Adam and Eve. You see, if God stayed in the perfect garden after tossing us sinners out and posting a guard at the gate to keep us out (a guard with a flaming sword, no less!), the Bible would be a lot shorter because the Bible is the account of God being with us no matter what. When we messed up and got ourselves evicted from paradise, God left the garden with us and stayed with us. The Bible is the story of God with us.

In Genesis 39, we read about the struggles Joseph went through after he was taken to Egypt by the traders who had bought him from his brothers. He ended up as a servant in the home of a prominent government official. After that official's wife accused Joseph of attacking her, Joseph was thrown into jail. Joseph had been a good kid. Perhaps he was a little arrogant, but he never did anything to deserve being trafficked as a slave or accused of rape. Nonetheless, he ended up in jail in a strange country with a strange language and no cell phone to call for help. Can you imagine the panic and the despair Joseph must have been feeling? The sense of aloneness?

Loneliness is a universal human emotion that is both complex and unique to each individual. Loneliness has a wide range of negative effects on both physical and mental health, including depression and suicide. Loneliness causes people to feel empty, alone, and unwanted. People who are lonely often crave human contact, but their state of mind makes it more difficult to form connections with other people.

Kovie Blakolo is a storyteller and writer from New York. In 2013, she wrote the piece "What Loneliness Feels Like."

Loneliness is a dark place. It's like sitting in a room at night by yourself and feeling like this is eternity. It's like being in a place with a thousand people but feeling invisible to every one of them. It's like walking on a path without any directions, without any idea when it will end.

Loneliness is feeling like you are meant to suffer alone; loneliness is suffering alone.

Loneliness is unnatural; human beings are to be in relationship. Loneliness is fear; there is no freedom in it. Loneliness is anxiety; worry its sister, uncertainty, its friend. Loneliness is endless wonder about endless wondering. Loneliness is cold with no hope for warmth but it is also unbearable heat. Loneliness is an awful paradox.

Loneliness is drowning in a sea or in a crowd of people. It is believing that your existence is insignificant; it is believing that you are meaningless to anyone and anything. Loneliness is tragedy; it is heartbreak and hardship and hurt. Loneliness is being covered in open wounds and scars that never heal. Loneliness is shame.

Loneliness is misery and sorrow; it is grieving with no hope. Loneliness is blinding and deafening. Loneliness is feeling unable. It is feeling discarded, unwanted, and unloved. Loneliness captivates nothing and no one. Loneliness is a bad dream but you cannot be awoken, you do not see the light of day.

Loneliness constricts the heart. Loneliness cripples the body and the mind and the soul. Loneliness is unconscious and numb. Loneliness is endless tears for change—any change that will tell you that you are alive. Because loneliness is dying at every moment; loneliness is death. (What

Loneliness Feels Like"; by Kovie Biakolo; April 7th 2013; The Thought Catalogue.com

I can imagine that this is what Joseph was feeling. But wait! Listen to this: While he was in jail, the Lord was with Joseph and remained loyal to him" (Genesis 39:21). God was with Joseph! In his darkest, most desperate moments, God was with Joseph. The promise that God is with us is threaded throughout the Bible. Over and over we are reminded that God is with us. That is a foundational promise!

> But Moses said to God, "Who am I to go to Pharaoh and to bring the Israelites out of Egypt?" God said, "I'll be with you." (Exodus 3:11–12)

Toward the end of his life, Moses said to the Israelites, "Be strong! Be fearless! Don't be afraid and don't be scared by your enemies, because the Lord your God is the one who marches with you. He won't let you down, and he won't abandon you" (Deuteronomy 31:6).

God said to Joshua, "I've commanded you to be brave and strong, haven't I? Don't be alarmed or terrified, because the Lord your God is with you wherever you go" (Joshua 1:9).

This thread continues into the New Testament.

The angel appeared to Joseph in his dream and said, "Look! A virgin will become pregnant and give birth to a son. And they will call him, 'Emmanuel'" (Matthew 1:23). Emmanuel means "God with us."

According to Matthew, Jesus's final words were, "I myself will be with you every day until the end of this present age" (Matthew 28:20).

There are so many more places in the scripture that reiterate this foundational principle, but Paul sums it up beautifully when he wrote to the church in Rome, "I'm convinced that nothing can separate us from God's love in Christ Jesus our Lord, not death or life, not angels or rulers, not present things or future things, not power or height or depth, or any other thing that is created" (Romans 8:38).

If you have ever felt utterly lost and alone, abandoned, forgotten, rejected, kicked out, or on your own with no map, and if you have ever experienced the depression that creeps over you following those feelings, then you are not alone in that experience. If you have ever lain in bed with the thought that you are not really the good person everyone else thinks you to be, and you have worried that someday "they" will discover the real you, but you don't even know who the real you is, welcome to the club! You'd be surprised at how many of us have been right there with you.

Now, imagine that you were taught that the God who created everything that exists no longer gives a flip about what happens in that creation. Imagine that God looks on earth or humanity only when he is angry or demands something from us. Imagine believing that we are on our own to figure things out and to find a way to recover from the dreadful mistakes we have made and will make because God has gone off somewhere else and isn't paying attention to us.

I think I would feel like crawling into a deep, dark hole and covering my head with my hands. If the only security I could expect were laws that told people not to hurt me, I would try to dig that hole deeper. I would be right there with Joseph in that Egyptian jail cell, wondering how much worse things could be.

One of the foundational principles of the Bible is that we are not alone; we have not been orphaned by an absentee parent. Our heavenly Father is with us. God is with us here, there, and everywhere. That is a foundation stone of our faith.

But I have never known someone in the grips of depression who has come out of it just because someone else said to them, "Get over it. You are not alone." The person who would give such glib advice has likely never felt the loneliness of their depressed friend. Words won't cure depression.

All the people in the Old Testament who were told, "God is with you," found it reassuring, I'm sure. But was it convincing? They still lost battles; they still lived under the rule of someone else. They still asked themselves, "If God is with us, where is he?"

To answer that question, God chose to come to us in our own form because God loves us so much that God didn't want there to be any doubt that he is with us.

In Romans 10:13–14, Paul mused, "All who call on the Lord's name will be saved. But how can they call on someone they don't have faith in? And how can they have faith in someone they haven't heard of? And how can they hear without a preacher?"

To that I would add that unless that preacher (ordained or not) who offers the counsel "You are not alone" is prepared to demonstrate with his or her own presence that the lonely and hurting one is not alone, then those words may well come across like a "clanging gong or clashing cymbal." (I Corinthians 13:1)

Paul knew that for the blessing "Christ be with you" to be real to a lonely, struggling person, it needed to be backed up by a physical presence. Thus he said to the church, "You are the body of Christ." (I Corinthians 12:27) Someone who is living in the darkness of loneliness and despair will need to feel the hand of Christ reaching out to embrace them and guide them and walk with them until they come to the realization that they are not alone. Now you are that hand. We who know Christ is with us are those hands that others desperately need to feel embracing them and lifting them up.

After having a discussion in a youth group one evening, on the promise that God is with you always, one of the boys—let's call him Todd—asked, "You mean that wherever I am and whatever I am doing, God is watching me?"

"Yes," I said.

"I don't like that," Todd replied. "It scares me to think that God is always spying on me. I don't want God to know everything I do."

I thought about saying, "Well, Todd, then be careful what you do." But I was able to stifle myself and say something more reassuring to that young man. (I don't remember now what it was, but Todd kept coming to the youth group, so I guess it wasn't too awful.)

I have often wondered what would elicit such a reaction from that teenage lad—"It scares me to know that God is spying on me." The best I can come up with is that in his experience, people who are watching you are watching to find you doing something wrong that they can fuss at you about or punish you for. I knew that in the church Todd was a part of, there was an ample number of adults who fit that description. I imagine that if Todd thought those "good Christian people" were like that, then he assumed God must be as well.

If we, who are God's church on earth today, don't want to teach people who are searching for a relationship with God that God is spying on them all the time, waiting to catch them doing something that he can punish them for, then we need to be careful that our encounters with people don't always end in some sort of judgment about them. Knowing that God is watching us all the time should be a comforting thought, not a scary image. More on that in chapter 4.

Moods
by George Appleton

O my Lord, when moods
of depression, anxiety, or loneliness
take possession of me,
let me ask, "Why art thou so heavy, O my soul,
and why art thou so disquieted within me?"

Then let your Spirit stir within me
to remind me that you are with me;
that you have not abandoned me,
and that you need me to be your presence
with those I know who are lonely.

Chapter 3

All Things Good

God works all things together for good.
—Romans 8:28

You planned something bad but God
produced something good from it.
—Genesis 50:20

LET'S GO BACK TO THE story of Joseph in Egypt. Last we heard, Joseph was languishing in an Egyptian jail.

Joseph was one of the twelve sons of Jacob (Israel) and one of only two sons of Jacob's favorite wife, Rachel. The brothers disliked Joseph because he was his father's favorite, and Joseph wouldn't let them forget it! They hatched a plan to sell him off to traveling merchants and tell their father that he had been killed by wild animals. They even spread the blood of a lamb on his "technicolor dream coat" and showed it to dear old Dad.

The traders who bought Joseph sold him to an

Egyptian, who put him to work around his estate. The man's wife tried to seduce Joseph, and when he wouldn't give in to her, she accused him of rape. Joseph ended up in jail for some time until he was summoned to the king to interpret a dream that greatly disturbed his royal majesty. You see, Joseph had already developed a reputation of interpreting the dreams of the other prisoners.

The king was impressed, and because his dream involved a coming time of national famine for seven years, the king not only released Joseph from jail but also put Joseph in charge of coordinating the stockpiling of food during the coming good years. He also made Joseph responsible for the distribution of food when the drought hit. When the seven lean years came, as predicted, Joseph was ready with enough food in the storehouses to feed the entirety of Egypt as well as people who came from all over pleading for help.

The famine spread up into Israel, where Joseph's family were among the starving. His father, Jacob (known as Israel by then), sent his sons to Egypt to beg for food. After a couple of trips, the brothers recognized that the Egyptian official they were dealing with was Joseph, that same snotty-nosed little brother whom they had sold to slave traders so many years before. "His brothers wept and said, 'Please forgive your brothers' sins and misdeeds, for they did terrible things to you. We are here as your slaves'"

"But Joseph said to them, 'Don't be afraid. Am I God? You planned something bad for me, but God produced something good from it, in order to save the lives of many people.'" (Genesis 50:17-18)

One way to understand this story would be to say that God set that whole plan in motion to save the children of Jacob/Israel, and that God had planned every detail of the saga. God knew a drought and famine would happen, so he put evil into the hearts of the brothers to position Joseph in a place where he could eventually provide food to his family. Therefore, the selling of Joseph into slavery was a "good thing" that was only much later recognized as good.

However, brothers selling a brother into slavery is a bad thing, no matter how you spin it! God doesn't do bad things, no matter what results from it. Those siblings had to live all those years under the cloud of guilt for what they had done. Perhaps not all the brothers were as willing to participate in the deed as others. If so, they lived knowing that they didn't do enough to stop an evil thing when they could have, which made them even guiltier. And their father had to live with the grief over the loss of a favorite child. What they did was a bad thing and not a good thing.

There was tension in that family, but by doing what they did, they bypassed all other options to work out or work through whatever issues were tearing apart the family. And if there was no other way to work things out, what about the less violent option of simply separating? That bad thing they did was in no way a good thing.

When we look at the whole story, what happened was that Joseph remained faithful to the God of his father and continued to work through his bad situation, trusting that

God had not abandoned him, until such time as he could do something to help others.

Joseph got married in Egypt. When Joseph and his wife had two sons, he named the first Manasseh, which means "God has helped me," and the second Ephraim, meaning "God has given me children in the land where I have been treated harshly" (Genesis 41:51–52). Even in the naming of his sons, we see Joseph giving praise to God.

Selling Joseph into slavery was a bad thing, but by staying close to his God and by serving others, the result was that something good came of it.

I know that a lot of folks think that Paul's words in Romans 8:28—"All things work together for good"—mean that somehow, there is a good thing embedded in every bad thing and that a bad thing can turn into a good thing if we trust God.

I disagree with that understanding of that passage.

When something bad happens, it is a bad thing. When a murder happens, that is an evil thing, and nothing will turn it into a good thing. When a child dies of cancer, that is a bad thing, and I don't know anything that could ever be said to those parents to make them think that it was a good thing. When a volcano erupts and buries a town in lava and ash, that is a terrible tragedy and a very bad thing, not a good thing in disguise. When Joseph's brothers sold him into slavery and lied to their father about what had happened to his son, that was a bad thing. There is no other way to spin it.

In Romans 8:28, Paul was not saying that "bad things become good things" but that by staying close to the God who is with us always, badness doesn't ever have to be the final result. Together with the guidance and council of the Holy Spirit, we can move past the hurt, pain, and guilt of the bad things to a place of peace and joy and hope. When we listen to and follow God's leading, the final result will always be good.

The thing about the foundational texts highlighted in this book is that they weave together like that "three-stranded cord" in Ecclesiastes to become a very sturdy foundation for our faith.

- All parts of creation are supremely good; God said so. Even storms and droughts are good. Storms are good because they replenish nutrients in the land. Droughts are good because they give the land a chance to lie fallow. All of the events of nature remind us that we don't control everything and are still dependent on the God of creation, and that the creation "is supremely good."

- God is with us, and nothing can separate us from God's love—not the violence of nature or the evil actions of others. God is with us always and does not abandon us.

- As God is with us, bad things are never the final things. In the symphony of life, bad things are but a prelude to good things for those who love and trust and work with God.

I have to tell you the story of Chris Downey, a blind architect.

At age forty-five, Chris Downey had pretty much constructed the life he'd always wanted. As an architect with a good job at a small housing firm outside San Francisco, he was happily married with a ten-year-old son. He was an assistant little league coach and avid cyclist. And then doctors discovered a tumor in his brain. The doctor told him that loss of sight was a possibility, but not to worry because the doctor had never had that happen. Chris had the surgery, and the tumor was safely gone—but he was left completely blind.

A month later, Chris returned to his office to try to figure out what to do next. Devastating, right? He was in a profession that depends on the ability to see because he needed to read blueprints and draw floor-plans. Chris reported that lots of people said, "That must be the worst thing imaginable—to be an architect and lose your sight!"

But Chris quickly came to realize that for him, the creative process is an intellectual process. It's how you think. He decided that he simply needed new tools. He found a printer that could emboss architectural drawings so that he could read and understand them through touch, like Braille.

When asked if he ever thought of his blindness as an insurmountable obstacle in his life, Downey said, "No. There was this sort of excitement, like I'm a kid again. I'm relearning so much of architecture. It wasn't about what I'm missing in architecture now; it's about what I had been missing in architecture before."

Chris began going to the Lighthouse for the Blind and learning how to figure out things in his new world.

Specifically, how to work in the kitchen safely, how to use screen-reading software to listen to emails as quickly as the rest of us read them, and how to navigate public transportation. "Blind people can do a lot of things. Driving isn't one of them! They don't like it when blind people drive," Chris says.

He seems to have a knack for finding windows when doors slam shut. Just nine months after going blind, the recession hit, and he lost his job. But he got word that a nearby firm was designing a rehabilitation center for veterans with sight loss, and they were eager to find a blind architect. What were the chances?

Chris said, "It seemed that the hand of God came down and took my disability and turned it upside down. All of a sudden I had a unique, unusual value that virtually nobody else had to offer."

Starting with that job, Downey developed a specialty: making spaces accessible to the blind. He helped design a new eye center at Duke University Hospital, he consulted on a job for Microsoft, and he signed on to help the visually impaired find their way in San Francisco's new, four-block-long Transbay Transit Center.

His biggest project yet, at the time of the *60 Minutes* report, was consulting on the total renovation of a new, three-story office space for his old training ground, the Lighthouse for the Blind.

Making a toast at a party celebrating his ten-year blind birthday, Chris said, "When you're fifty-five and you have a chance to be ten again, you take it!"

When asked if he thinks he may be a better architect

today, he said, "I'm absolutely convinced I'm a better architect today than I was sighted." (Adapted from the CBS TV show "60 Minutes", January 10, 2019.)

What caused Chris Downey to overcome the loss of sight in a job that "required" it? What gave this man the ability to go forward "in the darkness" and find the light of new possibilities and new opportunities? I believe the answer is simple. Chris never dwelt on the question "Why did this happen to me?" From the beginning of his ordeal, Chris focused on, "How can I find the way to something good through this? How can I make lemonade out of this boatload of lemons that has just fallen on me?"

Whenever life drops a load of lemons on you (or in my case, broccoli), you have the option of taking it personally and shouting out, "Why me? What did I do to deserve this? Why is God punishing me?" Or you can remember the foundations of our faith: the creation is supremely good, God is with you always, and no matter what happens, God will lead you past the bad to discover the good.

The bottom line is this:

> We know that God works all things together for good for the ones who love God, for those who are called according to his purpose... So what are we going to say about these things?" What we should say is, "If God is for us, [it doesn't matter] who is against us.... Who will separate us from Christ's love? Will we be separated by trouble, or distress, or harassment, or famine, or nakedness,

or danger, or sword? [No!] In all these things we win a sweeping victory through the one who loves us. I'm convinced that nothing can separate us from God's love in Christ Jesus our Lord: not death or life, not angels or rulers, not present things or future things, not powers or height or depth, or any other thing that is created. (Romans 8:28, 31, 35, 37–39)

With that in mind, we can draw strength and peace from the promise that all things—comfortable things or uncomfortable things, easy things or hard things, painful things or feel-good things—will work together for goodness when we trust God and seek his kingdom, not our personal fiefdoms.

Chapter 4

I Hear You

I've heard your cries of injustice.
—Exodus 2:24

"No man is an island," wrote John Donne in 1624. Yet from time to time, most of us have felt like we were on an island, so far from anyone who cared. We felt that no one could hear our cries for help, no one could see our pain. We have all known those times when we have shouted with our inner voices, "No one is listening to me! No one cares what I am feeling!"

Well, there is good news. In Exodus 2:23 we are told, "The Israelites cried out, and their cry to be rescued … rose up to God. God heard their cry of grief and God remembered his promise to their ancestors." In Exodus 3, God is speaking to Moses from the burning bush when God declares, "I've clearly seen my people oppressed in Egypt. I've heard their cry of injustice because of their slave masters. I know about their pain. I've come down to rescue them from the Egyptians" (Exodus 3:7). This promise is foundational to the entire message of the Bible!

By the early seventeenth century, the Renaissance movement was giving way to the Age of Enlightenment. The Age of Enlightenment, also known as the Age of Reason, was the time when people began to think! To question! To explore the world! To challenge ideas! To assert their own ideas!

One of the ideas that came under new scrutiny was the whole notion of, "What is God like?" For a long time, as a way of "controlling" the population, the Church promulgated the teaching that God was strict, punishing, and demanding. There were strict rules about sin and the chance of getting into heaven, and if you didn't follow them, you would go straight to hell.

It wasn't so much that people were challenging the existence of God, just the image of the God that the Church had been using to control their actions, their morality, and their dreams. Thinkers began to say things like, "Yes, of course there is a God—the creation is the evidence of God. But it makes no sense to believe that God is constantly interrupting our lives with painful, devastating events. We believe in God, but we don't believe that God interferes in our lives here on earth. That is why God gave us minds: so that we could figure things out and deal with whatever happens on our own."

Today, that theological position is known as deism. Deism refers to a belief in the existence of a supreme being who is regarded as the ultimate source of reality and ground of value but is not intervening in natural and historical processes by way of particular saving acts. Deists stress the importance of following reason. They are likely to express doubts about belief in mysteries such as the incarnation, the Trinity, and the reality of immortality. The foundational verses from Exodus say something different.

> The Israelites were still groaning because of their hard work. They cried out, and their cry to be rescued from the hard work rose up to God. God heard their cry of grief, and God remembered his covenant with Abraham, Isaac, and Jacob. God looked at the Israelites, and God understood. (Exodus 2:23b–25)

> Then the Lord said [to Moses], "I've clearly seen my people oppressed in Egypt. I've heard their cry of injustice because of their slave masters. I know about their pain. I've come down to rescue them from the Egyptians in order to take them out of that land and bring them to a good and broad land, a land that's full of milk and honey … Now the Israelites' cries of injustice have reached me. I've seen just how much the Egyptians have oppressed them. So get going. I'm sending you to Pharaoh to bring my people, the Israelites, out of Egypt." (Exodus 3:7–10)

The whole Bible story is built on the promise that God sees, God hears, and God comes down to do something!

And what God does is done, in part, through human agents. Moses wasn't the only person God called to help or lead God's people.

> After Moses died, the Lord spoke to Joshua … "My servant Moses is dead. Now get ready to cross over the Jordan with this entire people to the land that I am going to give to the Israelites … I will be with you in the same way I was with Moses. I won't desert you or leave you." (Joshua 1:1)

> The Lord was moved by Israel's groaning under those who oppressed and crushed them. So the Lord would raise up leaders for them, and the Lord would be with the leader, and he would rescue Israel from the power of their enemies. (Judges 2:18)

> [Isaiah said,] "The Lord God's spirit is upon me, because the Lord has anointed me. He has sent me to bring good news to the poor, to bind up the brokenhearted, to proclaim release for captives, and … to proclaim the year of the Lord's favor." (Isaiah 61:1–2a)

God always heard the cries of the people when they were in trouble. Every time God sent a Samson, a David, an Isaiah, or any of the other judges and prophets, God was responding to the cries and pains of God's people.

And then get ready for it, here it comes — God came himself!

God so loved the world that he gave his only Son,
so that everyone who believes in him won't perish
but will have eternal life. (John 3:16)

We'll talk more on John 3:16 in chapter 11.

God has come down to us in Moses, in the prophets,
in Jesus, in the Holy Spirit, and in the Church because
God loves the world, is aware of what is going on in
the world, and is committed to leading the world in the
direction of peace.

Remember Jesus saying, "I will not leave you orphans.
I will not leave you alone. I will be with you till the end
of time"? As I am writing this, the world is practically
on lockdown. A deadly virus is creeping through the
streets like the green death in the old *Ten Commandments*
movie! People are afraid. But the foundational verse for
this chapter says that God hears our cries and comes to
be with us, even now!

Now, I know what some of you are thinking. "If God
knows us and cares about us, why does God let bad things
happen to good people? Why doesn't God come down
and save me from all my trouble and pain and suffering?
If God knows what is going on in this world, why doesn't
God stop it? Or is God too busy to intervene in this
mess?" Am I right?

The first response to those questions that comes
to my mind is that God is not called according to our
purposes—we are called according to God's purpose.
God's purpose is to lead the whole world toward the light
of peace, to draw the world together in a community

of love. We are challenged by Jesus to "desire first and foremost God's kingdom (God's purpose) and not worry about the rest." (Matthew 6:33)

Second, we are not promised a rose garden. In fact, if you will remember, Jesus invited us to take up a cross and follow him. We are told that they abused and tortured Jesus, so why should we expect cotton candy and ice cream? We are promised a place in heaven, not a mansion on earth.

Third, God is love. God is always love. God is only love. God loves us before we even search for or are aware of God. God is good. All the time, God is good.

Those who blame God for bad things haven't met the God Jesus talked about. They don't understand the God that Jesus represents.

If we really believe these statements about God's love, then we must not forget them when something bad happens to us or to others. God isn't oblivious to our needs. God hears our cries. God doesn't cause hurt. God comes to us in the midst of our suffering. God doesn't hate, and God doesn't take out his anger on us. God loves. God loves us. God loves our enemies. God loves the worst sinner and felon. God loves you, and God loves me!

God always works for good and invites us to work for that good along with him. But we have the choice to do that or not. Sometimes the choices we make are uninformed, vindictive, or selfish, and those choices can lead to bad results. But those choices do not represent the will of God.

Sometimes the choices of others impact us. And some things that happen are just accidents. But neither our bad choices nor the bad choices of others are the work of God. The things we do that build a wall of separation between us and the constant love of God are our fault, not God's. But the promise is that whatever pain results from our bad choices or actions need not defeat us, because God is with us and heaven awaits us.

If the choices that bring bad didn't exist, Genesis wouldn't have God telling the residents of the garden, "Now you have a choice to eat of the fruit of the tree in the middle of the garden, or not. I am telling you not to, for your own good."

The life that God created for us comes with choices. Some lead to good things, and some lead to bad things. But even when we make the bad choices, or when bad things happen to us, we have the testimony of scripture that no matter what happens, God "hears our cries, sees our predicament, knows our pain, and comes to walk with us and lead us to a 'promised land,' a better place." God simply does not inflict bad things on the children God loves.

I don't know why some bad things happen. But as for me, I choose to praise God for everything good that happens to me, to you, and to the world. I choose to trust that when anything bad happens, God is with me, and together we can move on from the bad to find the good again. I will not blame God for anything bad!

After the Turbulence of the Day
by Helder Camara

After the turbulence of the day,
Thank you for sending the peacefulness of the night.
How blessed the peace of the night, so quiet, so still …

Let us not ruminate upon the
disagreeable scenes of the day.
Let us not rehearse injustices,
bitter, harsh words, or courses of action.

Mindful, Father, of your patience with us,
of your infinite goodness,
we ask you to help us never harbor a single drop
of hatred, or resentment, or bitterness
against anyone.

Fill us with your limitless mercy.

Chapter 5

If My People

If my people will humbly pray ...
—2 Chronicles 7:14

THE FOUNDATIONAL TEXT FOR THIS chapter is 2
Chronicles 7:14.

> *If my people who belong to me will humbly pray,*
> *seek my face, and turn from their wicked ways, then*
> *I will hear from heaven, forgive their sin, and heal*
> *their land.*

There is some background that will be helpful in fully
appreciating the meaning of these divine words. Let me
set the stage.

The book of 2 Chronicles tells the story from the
building of Solomon's temple until the time of the
destruction of that temple by Babylon. When David died,
his son Solomon became king. Solomon got off to a good
start. He asked God only for "wisdom and knowledge"

(2 Chronicles 1:10) so he could lead the nation. Because Solomon had not asked for "wealth, riches, fame, or victory over those who [hated him], or even for a long life," (2 Chronicles 1:11) God agreed to grant Solomon's prayer for wisdom and knowledge. Solomon also ended up with some pretty fabulous riches and women!

Then Solomon committed to building a "magnificent" temple to God—and, by the way, a royal palace for himself! He imported the timber from Tyre, in Lebanon, along with craftsmen expert in working with wood, gold, silver, bronze, iron, fabrics, and yarns.

A hint of the competitive personality of Solomon peeks through in the letter he wrote to the king of Tyre requesting the materials for the temple. Solomon told king Hiram, "The temple I am about to build must be magnificent, because our God is greater than all other gods!" And, indeed, Solomon made sure that the temple he was building would be the greatest the world had ever seen.

I'm going to go get a snack now while I give you time to read the descriptions of the temple in 2 Chronicles 3–4. Take your time and imagine what it must have looked like.

Wow! Quite opulent, right? Over the top, one might say. We have a wonderfully beautiful church where I attend, but it is nothing like this! Solomon and all the people were rightfully proud of what they had built to the glory of God as a statement to everyone else that "Our God is better than your God" (Nyah, nyah, nyah, nyah, nyah!).

The Jewish historian Josephus, writing for the Roman Empire, gives this description of Solomon's temple:

> [The ceiling] had plates of gold nailed upon them; and as he enclosed the walls with boards of cedar, so he fixed on them plates of gold, which had sculptures upon them; so that the whole temple shined, and dazzled the eyes of such as entered, by the splendor of the gold that was on every side of them.
>
> Now the whole structure of the temple was made with great skill of polished stones, and those laid together so very harmoniously and smoothly that there appeared to the spectators no signs of any hammer, or other instrument of architecture, but as if, without any use of them, the entire materials had naturally united themselves together that the agreement of one part with another seemed rather to have been natural, than to have arisen from the force of tools upon them ...
>
> He also laid the floor of the temple with plates of gold; and he added doors to the gate of the temple, and on them he attached gold plates; and to say all in one word, he left no part of the temple but was covered with gold."

— *Josephus Complete Works; The Antiquities of the Jews;* by Flavius Josephus; Translated by William Whiston; Kregel Publications; Grand Rapids, Michigan; Book III; Selected from pages 174-176)

When the temple was complete, they held a weeklong dedication ceremony. In chapter 5 of 2 Chronicles, we read that they brought to the new temple all the items that David had accumulated for the worship center—or at least all the gold and silver items. Then they brought up the chest containing the tablets of the law Moses received from God: the Ark of the Covenant. When the chest was in place, they sacrificed "countless sheep and oxen" to consecrate the spot.

Don't forget that these slaughtered animals were their livelihood, the product of their labor—sheep for wool and meat and milk, and oxen to pull the plows and wagons. You don't replace a full-grown ox very rapidly. These were significant sacrifices.

Everyone was there! All the priests, all the tribes, the Levites, and the royal family dressed in their finest clothes. There were bands with trumpets, cymbals, harps, and zithers, and brass—over a hundred trumpets! And there was a choir of hundreds singing, "Yes, God is good! God's faithful love lasts forever" (2 Chronicles 5:12–13).

You can imagine the scene: cheering and dancing, children running around and screaming, animals bellowing, the smells of a barbeque filling the air, and hawkers trying to sell souvenirs or fried dates on a stick. It was a party like no other!

Then with the band playing, the choir singing, and the fires from the altar blazing, "the Lord's glory filled the temple" in the form of a cloud so thick that "the priests were unable to carry out their duties on account of the cloud" (2 Chronicles 5:14).

Solomon addressed the gathered nation and reminded them that God had selected him for the honor of building the temple (2 Chronicles 6:3).

Solomon climbed the steps of a bronze platform he had built and placed in the middle of the courtyard so all could see him. He turned to face the altar and knelt with his arms outstretched and began to pray. It is the form of his prayer that gets us to our foundational verse for today (2 Chronicles 6:13).

The text of Solomon's prayer is found in 2 Chronicles 6:4–42. It is a long passage but worth reading, so let me lift up just some of its passages.

> So now, Lord God of Israel, keep what you promised my father David your servant. (6:16)

> Lord, my God, listen to your servant's prayer and request, and hear the cry and prayer that I your servant pray to you. (6:19)

> Listen to the request of your servant and your people Israel when they pray ... Listen from your heavenly dwelling place, and when you hear, forgive! (6:21)

> When your people go to war against their enemies, wherever you may send them, and they pray to you toward this city ... then listen from heaven to their prayer and [their] request and do what is right for them. (6:34)

Did you pick up on a theme there? "God, you see the wonderful thing we have done here—all the work, all the marble, all the gold, and all in your name? Now, God listen to us. Here's what we want you to do … God, do this … God, do that." That is rather demanding, don't you think?

Following the prayer, God's spirit again filled the temple with his glory, and all the people fell to their faces "worshipping and giving thanks to the Lord saying, 'God is good all the time and all the time, God is good!'" Then they sacrificed 22,000 oxen and 120,000 sheep while the band played on.

Almost 150,000 animals! They had to move the ceremony outside because the courtyard inside wasn't big enough. The sacrificing and dedicating went on for a week; I guess it took that long to barbeque all that meat! Then the party continued for another week! (2 Chronicles 7:7–9)

> On the twenty-third day of the seventh month, Solomon dismissed the people to their tents, happy and content because of the goodness the Lord had shown to David, to Solomon, and to his people Israel. In this way, Solomon finished the Lord's temple and the royal palace. He successfully accomplished everything he intended for the Lord's temple and his own palace. (2 Chronicles 7:10–11)

I imagine Solomon was feeling pretty pleased with himself for having built God a showplace temple and displaying his respect with all the gold and silver and fine woodwork, and with the grand dedication ceremony and celebration. It must have been hard for him to sleep that night with his arm still bent over his shoulder patting himself on the back!

> Then the Lord appeared to Solomon at night and said to him: "I have heard your prayer and have chosen this place as my house of sacrifice. When I close the sky so that there is no rain or I order the locusts to consume the land or I send a plague against my people, if my people who belong to me will [humble themselves] and pray, seek my face, and turn from their wicked ways, then I will hear from heaven, forgive their sins, and heal their land." (2 Chronicles 7:12–14)

It sounds like God appreciated the effort that they had put into building the temple and making it so beautiful, but is that what God really wanted from his people? What can we do to please God? We can humble ourselves, pray, seek the face of God, and turn from wickedness. This is the foundational text for this chapter.

What does God want from us?

> I desire faithful love and not sacrifice (of 150,000 animals), the knowledge of God instead of entirely burned offerings. (Hosea 6:6)

What can we do to please God?

> He has told you, human one, what is good and
> what the Lord requires from you, to do justice,
> embrace faithful love, and walk humbly with your
> God. (Micah 6:8)

Let's take a closer look at that foundational verse in 2 Chronicles.

"If my people who are called by my name"

Whom is God talking about? God is talking about people who identify themselves as believers, as the righteous, as God's own people. Wait a minute! That's us, isn't it? We call ourselves by the name of God's own Son; we claim to be "Christ's Ones." We are the ones who gather weekly to bow before God, to sing praise to God, to listen to God. We are God's people. God is talking to us! So how do we honor our God? How do we receive the peace that God offers?

"If we will humble ourselves"

Humility is assuming a deferential respect, assuming a position of meekness or modesty. The person who acts as though he or she needs no help is not humble. Those who believe that they are sufficient unto themselves are not humble. The person who goes through life without seeking or accepting help from God or anyone else is not humble and fails to meet the first criterion for receiving God's peace.

"If we will humble ourselves and pray" and *"If we will humbly pray"*

Prayer is our way of sending a spiritual text message to God to say, "Thank you," and, "I could use your guidance and help." If we don't pray, we are declaring that we don't need God or God's help for our living. The person who does not pray is not humble.

Humble prayer is prayer that is not constantly asking for things for myself. Humble prayer is prayer that expresses concern for others—for other people and other nations. Humble prayer is prayer that earnestly seeks to know what is the will of God and desires for God's will to be done, pleasurable to me or not. Humble prayer is prayer in which I offer myself to do and to suffer for others. John Wesley's covenant prayer is a beautiful example of humble prayer.

> I am no longer my own, but thine.
> Put me to what thou wilt, rank me with whom
>   thou wilt.
> Put me to doing, put me to suffering.
> Let me be employed by thee or laid aside for thee,
> Exalted for thee or brought low for thee.
> Let me be full, let me be empty.
> Let me have all things, let me have nothing.
> I freely and heartily yield all things to thy pleasure
>   and disposal.
> And now, O Glorious and blessed God,
> Father, Son, and Holy Spirit,

> Thou art mine, and I am thine. So be it.
> And the covenant which I have made on earth,
> Let it be ratified in heaven. Amen.

"If my people will seek my face"

Are you seeking the face of God? Have you found it? Let me share with you some of the words of a true saint in whose time we were all privileged to have lived: Mother Teresa of the Sisters of Charity.

> The Missionaries of Charity do firmly believe that they are touching the body of Christ in his distressing disguise whenever [we] are helping and touching the poor. We cannot do this with a long face. We cannot do it just [because], because it is to Jesus that we are doing it. The whole of our [little] society is engaged in doing just that: feeding the hungry of Christ, clothing the naked of Christ, taking care of the sick of Christ, and giving a home to the homeless Christ.
>
> Once, before sending a group of new sisters to the Home for the Dying, Mother Teresa told them, "You [have seen] the priest during Mass: with what love, with what delicate care he touched the body of Christ [in the sacrament]! Make sure you do the same thing when you go to the Home for the Dying, for Jesus is there in the distressing disguise." And so they went.
>
> [Upon their return, she] asked the sisters:

"What did you feel when you were touching the poor?" One of the sisters answered her question [for all the others], "I have never felt the presence of Christ so real, as when I was touching them."

The poor do us the honor of allowing us to [see the face of God in] them.

—Mother Teresa of Calcutta, *My Life for the Poor*, (San Francisco, Harper & Row,1985, page 18-19.

Where do you see the face of God? Are you searching for it?

"If my people will turn from their wicked ways"

"Wicked ways" says more than just the "common, little sins" that we all commit daily. Wickedness is greater than that! Wickedness is deep-seated hatred, intolerance, and injustice. Injustice is the systemic, unfair treatment of others born out of hatred and prejudice.

In the words of Martin Luther King Jr., in his letter from the Birmingham Jail, "Injustice anywhere is a threat to justice everywhere. We are caught in an inescapable network of mutuality, tied in a single garment of destiny. Whatever affects one directly, affects all indirectly."

Are our beautiful sanctuaries and elaborate worship services all that God wants from us?

Take away the noise of your songs, I won't listen to the melody of your harps. But let justice roll down like waters, and righteousness like an ever flowing stream. (Amos 5:23–24)

What does God most want from the people "who are called by his name"? To do justice, to let justice "roll down like waters." To treat others with respect, fairness, and compassion, without judgment or oppression. Not to take a "better than thou" attitude toward others, but to see each person as a beloved child of the God to whom we pray.

Through the prophet Isaiah, God spoke the following words.

> I am fed up with your burnt offerings of rams and the fat of well-fed beasts. I don't want the blood of bulls, lambs, and goats … Stop bringing worthless offerings. Your incense repulses me. I can't stand wickedness with celebrations! … When you extend your hands, I'll hide my eyes from you. Even when you pray for a long time, I won't listen. Your hands are stained with blood … Wash! Be Clean! Remove your ugly deeds from my sight. Put an end to such evil; Learn to do good. Seek justice: help the oppressed; defend the orphan; plead for the widow. (Isaiah 1:11–17)

And from the New Testament:

> True [worship], the kind that is pure and faultless before God the Father, is this: to care for orphans

and widows in their difficulties and to keep the world from contaminating us. (James 1:27)

It is a foundational principle of the Bible that "not everyone who says, 'Lord, Lord' enters the kingdom of heaven, but those who do what is God's will," and that will is to "seek the face of God, to pray humbly, to turn from our wicked and unjust ways, to do justice, to love mercy, and to care for the orphans, the widows, the hungry and the hurting." It is repeated throughout the Bible from God's word to Solomon to Jesus' words to us.

To put it in contemporary terms, we must not only talk the talk of devotion to our God; we must walk the walk of love for all those whom God loves.

God honored the building of the magnificent temple of Solomon by saying,

> I have heard your prayer and have chosen this place as my house ... From now on my eyes will be open and my ears will pay attention to the prayers offered in this place, because I have chosen this temple and declared it holy so my name may be there forever. My eyes and my heart will always be there. (2 Chronicles 7:12–16)

We all pray that God has said the same thing about the beautiful temples we have built to his name and where we worship and offer praise. But let us not forget that what God really desires from us is to "seek his face" and not the face of any lesser god, "to humbly walk with him," to "humbly pray to him," asking not for ourselves but for others, and "to turn from our wicked ways" and follow the path of Jesus, his Son and our Savior.

"Lord, Open Our Eyes"
by Mother Teresa of Calcutta

Lord, open our eyes,
    that we may see you in our brothers and sisters.
Lord, open our ears,
    that we may hear the cries of the hungry, the cold,
    the frightened, the oppressed.
Lord, open our hearts,
    that we may love each other as you love us.
Renew in us your spirit
Lord, free us and make us one.

Chapter 6

My Shepherd

I am the good shepherd.
—John 10 11

The Lord is my shepherd, I lack nothing.
He leads me in grassy meadows;
he leads me to restful waters;
he keeps me alive.
He guides me in proper paths for
the sake of his good name.

Even when I walk through the darkest valley,
I fear no danger because you are with me.
Your rod and your staff—they protect me

You set a table for me right in front of my enemies.
You bathe my head in oil; my cup is so full it spills over!

Yes, goodness and faithful love will
pursue me all the days
of my life,
and I will live in the Lord's house as long as I live.
(Psalm 23)

I HAVE SELECTED PSALM 23 as one of the foundational texts of the Bible not so much because everyone knows it and it is a beloved text, but because the images it so beautifully and poetically presents are significant and important to the overall message of the entire Bible. They are metaphors that contradict so much of what passes as pop or common theology. As beautiful as these images are, they become even more foundational and helpful the more we know about them, particularly about sheep and shepherds (about which, thanks to the Internet, I know a great deal!).

This psalm has to do with the relationship that exists between ourselves and the eternal God of our faith. Sadly, for so many people, that relationship is summed up in just a few negative words: "God is big and powerful and scary." "God is demanding and gets violently angry when he doesn't get what he wants from us." "We are so bad that we are always disappointing and angering God, and that brings the wrath of God down on us." "We are doomed!"

That expression of theology is a remnant of a very sincere effort on the part of the Church in ages gone by. In taking seriously the responsibility to protect the uneducated populace from themselves, they threatened them with God's wrath if they got out of line. It was really the same tactic that parents use when trying to protect their children from the stupid and dangerous choices they are prone to make.

We've all said things like, "If you cheat at school, you'll never get a good job!" Or, after repeated warnings, "If you do that again, you will never leave this house again!" Our protective intentions are good, but they can result in a child who is afraid to do anything on their own, or a child who one day realizes the emptiness of that kind of threat and loses respect for the parent.

What the Church intended to communicate, I believe, was, "Life will be better with less friction among neighbors if you will live according to the commands of God, because what God really desires is for you to have an abundantly fulfilling life." Psalm 23 presents our relationship with God in a much more positive and hopeful way than what many people believe.

The psalm is attributed to King David. In his younger years, David was a shepherd in the hills around Bethlehem, his hometown. When David volunteered to fight the giant, Goliath, King Saul said to David, "You can't go out and fight this Philistine, you are still a boy!" (1 Samuel 17:33).

> "Your servant has kept his father's sheep," David replied to Saul, "and if ever a lion or a bear came and carried off one of the flock, I would go after it, strike it, and rescue the animal from its mouth. If it turned on me, I would grab it at its jaw, strike it, and kill it. Your servant has fought both lions

and bears. This uncircumcised Philistine will be just like one of them because he has insulted the army of the living God." "The Lord," David added, "who rescued me from the power of both lions and bears, will rescue me from the power of this Philistine." (1 Samuel 17:34–37)

Now, I am a city boy, and all I really know about sheep is that wool clothes itch! So I looked up some facts that helped me gain a deeper understanding of the images in the psalm.

Fun Facts about Sheep

- There are approximately one billion sheep worldwide and about nine hundred different breeds.
- Sheep have best friends! Just like you and me, sheep form close bonds with other sheep.
- Sheep have excellent memories. They can remember individual sheep and humans for years.
- Sheep know how you feel. Sheep display emotions, some of which can be studied by observing the position of their ears (like cats). They also display and recognize emotion by facial expressions.
- Sheep are famously friendly. Sheep wag their tails like dogs, they know their names, and

they form strong bonds with other sheep, goats, and people.

"Contrary to popular misconception," said one article, "Sheep are extremely intelligent animals capable of problem solving. They are considered to have a similar IQ level to cattle and are nearly as clever as pigs." High praise!

Another article describes sheep in far less glowing words:

> Sheep are dumb and directionless. They are also defenseless. Left to themselves, sheep will not and cannot last very long. Just about any other domesticated animal can be returned to the wild and will stand a fighting chance of survival. But not sheep. Put a sheep in the wild and you've just given nature a snack."

Think about it. There are different ways animals react when they perceive some kind of danger. Three common ones are fight, flight, and posturing.

Let's think about fight. A sheep gets frightened or sees that he is in danger. Maybe he sees a bear rambling toward him. What is he going to do? He doesn't have claws, he doesn't have fangs, he doesn't have venom, and he doesn't have spines or quills or large talons. He's got nothing to protect himself. Fighting is definitely out. But that's okay; there are lots of other animals that don't fight it out.

How about flight—just turning tail and running away? That's a good defense mechanism. Unfortunately, sheep aren't fast. They certainly aren't agile, especially when their wool is long, and even more so when their wool is long and wet. Last I checked, they don't have wings. A sheep is not going to outrun or outfly a bear. The sheep will not fight and it cannot take flight. (So far it is looking pretty good for the bear.)

How about posturing? A dog will bark and growl and show his teeth to warn you away. A lion will roar. A rattlesnake will shake his rattle. A cat will arch his back and hiss. The best a sheep can do is baa. I don't think that bear is going be too intimidated.

It is for good reason that no one relies on a guard sheep to keep one's property secure. Sheep can't fight, they can't run away, and they can't scare away. So what does a sheep do when danger comes? It flocks. When a bear approaches, the sheep will gather with others in a pack and run in circles in complete panic, hoping that the bear will choose someone else. Without a shepherd to protect them, they'll be picked off and eaten one by one.

Why is it helpful to know something about sheep? Because when David writes, "The Lord is my shepherd," you can't miss the inference: "I am like a sheep."

We are like sheep. We can't survive for very long on our own without falling prey to predators, wandering away and getting hopelessly lost, or injuring ourselves through our own stubbornness or stupidity.

> Sheep are dumb and directionless and defenseless. So I guess when God says that we are sheep who need a shepherd, he doesn't mean it as a compliment to us. It is just a very realistic assessment of who

we are and what we need. We are sheep who are completely dependent upon a shepherd.

—Tim Challies, "Dumb, Directionless, Defenseless," August 26, 2013

But "the Lord is my shepherd." God is like a shepherd. So what is a shepherd like? We know from Jesus himself that there are good shepherds, and there are bad shepherds:

"I am the good shepherd. The good shepherd lays down his life for the sheep. When the hired hand sees the wolf coming, he leaves the sheep and runs away. That's because he isn't the shepherd; the sheep aren't really his. So the wolf attacks the sheep and scatters them. He's only a hired hand and the sheep don't matter to him.

I am the good shepherd. I know my own sheep and they know me, just as the Father knows me and I know the Father. I give up my life for the sheep. I have other sheep that don't belong to this fold. I must lead them too. They will listen to my voice and there will be one flock, with one shepherd. (John 10:11–16)

Beth Greenwood wrote an article titled "What Are the Duties of a Shepherd" on June 28, 2018.

Most shepherds take care of sheep, although they may be responsible for goats as well. They often work in isolated areas and may work independently except for the assistance of herding or guard dogs. Many sheepherders must be on call for their animals around the clock.

A shepherd's primary responsibility is the safety and welfare of the flock. Some flocks may include as many as 1,000 sheep. The shepherd will graze the animals, herding them to areas of good forage, and keeping a watchful eye out for poisonous plants. As the sheep eat all the forage in an area, the shepherd will move both the sheep and his living quarters to fresh range. In most cases, the shepherd and his dogs will move the sheep out to fresh grazing each day and bring them back to bed down in the same area each night.

To protect the sheep under his care, a shepherd may use guard dogs or other guard animals. Sheep predators include coyotes, wolves, mountain lions, bears and domestic dogs, according to the U.S. Department of Agriculture. In addition to using guard animals, many sheepherders carry [weapons to defend against] predators that are attacking the sheep.

Like other animals, sheep are susceptible to diseases, and they must also be monitored during the lambing process. They may also be bothered by insects, some of which carry disease. Shepherds are often responsible for minor injuries or basic medical treatment, especially since they work in isolated areas far from veterinary services.

Unlike other animals that shed their hair in

the spring, many breeds of sheep must be shorn. Shearing must be practiced for the health and hygiene of each individual animal. Unlike other animals, most sheep are unable to shed. This can cause sheep to become overheated and die. Urine, feces and other materials that become trapped in the wool attract flies, maggots and other pests. An experienced shepherd is able to shear the animal without nicking or cutting the skin, and to remove the fleece intact.

David, in trying to express his deep faith in the God of his fathers, reflects back on something he knows well: the attributes and skills of a good shepherd.

"He lets me rest in grassy meadows"

I assume that most rural pasture lands are much like my yard: not everything that is green is grass! Sheep aren't discerning eaters. They will eat whatever is under their noses. And they will continue to eat in one place until all the grass and the roots of the grass are gone, and they are left eating dirt—or so I have read.

God leads us to pastures of goodness and gives us time to rest there, out of danger and with abundant provision for our needs.

"He leads me to restful waters"

Sheep are so easily frightened that they can be sent into a panic by the noise and confusion of rapidly running waters. They won't drink from a disturbed river, and they won't know where to go to find calm, fresh waters.

The Good Shepherd has to lead them. The Good Shepherd leads us to safe places, refreshing places. God, our Good Shepherd, has given us the testimony of the scriptures to lead us. And God gives us, every moment, his Holy Spirit to instruct us and guide us to places of beauty and restoration—places where we can recharge and restart and go on with strength.

> Contrary to the usual understanding, the imagery in vv. 2–3 is not aimed primarily at communicating a sense of peace and tranquility. It does this, to be sure, but its primary intent is to say that God keeps the psalmist alive. For a sheep, to be able to "lie down in green pastures" means to have food; to be led "beside still waters" means to have something to drink; to be led "in right paths" means that danger is avoided and proper shelter is attained. In short, God "restores my soul," or, better translated, God "keeps me alive." The sheep lack nothing because the shepherd provides the basic necessities of life—food, drink, shelter. Thus the psalmist professes that his or her life depends solely on God and that God keeps the psalmist alive "for his name's sake"—that is, in keeping with God's fundamental character.
>
> —New Interpreters Bible vol. 4, p. 767–68

"Even when I walk through the darkest valley, I fear no danger because you are with me"

There it is again: God is with me. Even in the bad times, God is with me. Even in the dark times, God is with me. Even in the scary times, God is with me.

As we drove through the area, there is a place along the road through the Sinai Desert that we were told is called the Valley of Death. Along that section of road, the terrain is steep on either side of the road, and there are several sharp twists and turns in the road that prevent a traveler from seeing what lies ahead. It feels like you are driving through a canyon. The guide told us that in the past that place was a known hangout for highway robbers, who would pounce on a caravan from the steep clifftops. Given the fact that we had a heavily armed guard on the bus with us, I wondered just how far in the past those times were.

But no armed guard and no high-powered weapon can protect us from the ever-looming prospect of death that all of us face. That is why that phrase begins with the word "even," because there is no escaping it. We will all pass through that dark valley.

But even when we walk that part of the road, we need fear no danger because God is with us and will use all the weapons at his disposal to protect us and guide us through. God will not turn and run away like the bad shepherd Jesus spoke of, because the bad shepherd "is just a hireling, the sheep aren't his and they don't matter to him" (John 10:12–13). "But we are his people, the sheep of his pasture" (Psalm 100:3).

"You set a table for me right in front of my enemies"

This is one of those places where it is important to note what the text doesn't say. David doesn't say, "You will take all my enemies away." There will be enemies and opponents, those who will slander us and revile us and even persecute us both emotionally and physically. But again, God is with us, and God will provide for our needs. God doesn't back down from those who hate him. They don't scare God. God loves even them.

"You bathe my head in oil; my cup is so full it spills over"

These are the expected acts of a hospitable host: to feed, to wash, and to offer more than sufficient water in the dryness of the desert. The Good Shepherd does not fail to care for the sheep, even in the very face of enemies. Enemies don't faze the Good Shepherd!

"Surely goodness and mercy shall follow me all the days of my life"

The Common English Bible translates the Hebrew verb *follow* with its more active sense of *pursue*.

"Yes, goodness and faithful love will pursue me all the days of my life"

God is in active pursuit of the psalmist! This affirmation is particularly noteworthy in view of "the presence of my enemies." Ordinarily in the psalms, it is precisely the enemies who "pursue" the reader (cf. 7:5; 71:11; 109:16). Here the enemies are present but have been rendered harmless while God is in active pursuit.

—New Interpreters Bible, vol. 4, 768)

"And I will live in the Lord's house as long as I live"

The exact Hebrew translation is "for the length of days." As Christians, we can't read this closing line but through the lens of the New Testament. There are signs of the hope of eternal life in the Old Testament—for example, in Daniel 12:2.

> Many of those who sleep in the dusty land will wake up—some to eternal life, others to shame and eternal disgrace. Those skilled in wisdom will shine like the sky. Those who lead many to righteousness will shine like the stars forever and always.

But in the New Testament, that hope is turned into a promise with the rising of Jesus from the dead! And in some of his final words to his church, Jesus referred to "his father's house," in which there will be a room prepared and ready for each one who lives and believes in him.

Jesus said, "I am the good shepherd. The good shepherd lays down his life for the sheep."

What more could we ask for than a shepherd who provides rest and guidance along the best paths? He is a shepherd who protects us from foes and, even in the moment of death, stays with us and protects us? A shepherd who invites us to the banquet at his table, bathes us in his love, and fills us to overflowing with his goodness. A shepherd who will pursue us even when we deliberately wander away from his embrace. A shepherd who prepares a place for us in his house, where we will live forever!

There is nothing more we could ask for. "The Lord is my shepherd. I shall not want for anything." "With the Lord as my shepherd, there is nothing needed that I lack!" This is foundational because it so lyrically describes the God of the whole Bible.

Psalm 25

I offer my life to you, Lord.
My God, I trust you.
Make your ways known to me, Lord;
teach me your paths.
Lead me in your truth—
teach it to me because you are the God who saves me.
I put my hope in you all the day long.
Remember me only according to your faithful love
for the sake of your goodness, Lord.
Please, for the sake of your good name,
Lord, forgive my sins, which are many.
Turn to me, God,
and have mercy on me.

Let integrity and virtue guard me
because I hope in you.
Please, God, save [your people]
from all our troubles!
Amen.

Chapter 7

What God Wants

JUST BEFORE CHRISTMAS, LITTLE JESSICA asked her daddy, "Christmas is Jesus' birthday, right, Daddy?"

"Yes, sweetheart, it is."

"Well, I want to get Jesus a birthday present."

"That's a good idea. Why don't you go make something for him?"

"But I don't know what Jesus wants from me."

And there it is! At some point, in some way, we all come up against the question, "What does Jesus want from me?" After we meet and fall in love with Jesus, we realize that we want to please him—but how? Even if our religion just centers on a belief that there is a divine, all-powerful creator, we want to please so as to not incur his anger. How? How do we do that?

"What does God want from me?" That's a question that cuts through a lot of questions and concerns related to our faith. We can learn all about the stories of the heroes of old. We can hear the sermons of the great rabbis and apostles. We can know the parables of Jesus. But just what are we supposed to do? How are we supposed to act to show our devotion to God? What does God want from us?

There are old laws that spell out how many steps you can take on a given day, or what you can and cannot eat for breakfast, or what cloth your shirt can be made of. Is that what God wants? And there are newer rule books that dictate what time of day you should pray, which direction on the compass you should face when you pray, what position you should assume when you pray, how you should hold your hands when you pray, and whether you should say "amen" at the end of your prayers? Is that what we must do to please God?

There are other issues that I should perhaps be careful about if I am going to do what God wants me to do. What occupation should I pursue? What denomination should I join? How should I vote? Can I dance? (Actually, no, *I* can't dance. But you get the point.) What does God want from me? How can I know?

Selecting the foundational text for this chapter was made easier when I came across the words of Psalm 89:14, and Psalm 97:2—"Righteousness and justice are the foundation of [God's] throne" (NRSV).

In reality, there are a number of foundational texts for this chapter.

> Sow for yourselves righteousness and reap steadfast love. (Hosea 10:12)

> Hold fast to justice and wait continually for your God. (Hosea 12:6)

The prophet Micah asks and answers our exact question:

> What does the Lord require of you?—To do justice and to love kindness and walk humbly with your God. (Micah 6:8)

Amos said the same thing a little more poetically.

> Let justice roll down like waters, and righteousness like an ever-flowing stream. (Amos 5:24)

Jeremiah expands the same thought with these words:

> Do what is just and right; rescue the oppressed from the power of the oppressor. Don't exploit or mistreat the refugee, the orphan, and the widow. Don't spill the blood of the innocent. (Jeremiah 22:3)

Jesus entered the discussion when chastising the religious leaders in his day.

> Woe to you, scribes and Pharisees, hypocrites! For you tithe mint, dill, and cumin, and you have neglected the weightier matters of the law: justice and mercy and faith. It is these you ought to have practiced. (Matthew 32:23)

Tithing mint, dill, and cumin are part of that old rule book of things you must do to please God. But Jesus is saying that there are more fundamental things that we should be doing than counting out mint and dill leaves and cumin seeds.

Let's talk about justice and righteousness because they are the "foundation of the throne of God" and are what Jesus says we should be practicing. In the Old Testament alone, the words *justice* and *righteousness* are coupled together thirty times!

> The Lord says [of Abraham], "I have chosen him, that he may charge his children and his household after him to keep the way of the Lord by doing righteousness and justice." (Genesis 18:19)

> Give the king your justice, O God, and your righteousness to a king's son. May he judge your people with righteousness, and your poor with justice. (Psalm 72:1–2)

> Thus says the Lord, "Maintain justice and do what is right, for soon my salvation will come, and my deliverance be revealed. Happy is the mortal who does this." (Isaiah 56:1)

Most of the time when we hear about justice, someone is talking about the justice system—courts, laws, trials, evidence, verdicts, and judgments. We hear from people who have been victimized by crime saying, "All we want is justice for our loved one," meaning, "All we want is for the accused to be punished. That will be justice." (Actually, I think that what most of the people who say things like that are really saying is, "Unless the court punishes that scumbag the way I think he should be punished, there won't be any justice!") In this way, justice is something taken from someone who has taken something from a victim.

That is certainly one aspect of the concept of justice: impartial arbitration between two parties. But that is not the only one. Referring to the justice system depersonalizes the concept of justice. It turns justice into an unpredictable result someone receives because of what was done to them.

But there is another manifestation of justice: justice as something I give to another not because I owe it to them or because it is demanded of me, but as a result of the love and reverence with which I hold them. Justice that comes from me and is not something imposed on you.

Jesus spoke to this new idea about justice when he said, "Don't even begin to think that I have come to do away with the law and the prophets." (Those old rules.) "I have not come to do away with them, but to fulfill them." And how does he intend that they should be fulfilled?

> A legal expert tested him, "Teacher, what is the greatest commandment in the Law?"[Jesus] replied, "You must love the Lord your God with all your heart, with all your being, and with all your mind. This is the first and greatest commandment. And the second is like it: You must love your neighbor as you love yourself. All the law and the prophets depend on these two commands." (Matthew 22:35–40)

Chapter 8

Every Sin Forgiven

People will be forgiven for every sin.–
—Matthew 12:31

WE ALL WORRY ABOUT SIN—AND well we should! Sin is hurtful, destroys good relationships, and causes pain. The effects of sin can spread like a pandemic, causing damage to innocent bystanders. Sin creates victims and debilitates its purveyors. We can thank Paul for the reminder that "All of us have sinned and fall short of the glory of God" (Romans 3:22).

The problem with sin is, What can we do about this terrible situation we have gotten ourselves into? We have not done God's will. We have broken God's law. We have not loved our neighbors. We have not heard the cry of the needy. We are surely in trouble! What can we do?

How can we get back on God's good side? How can we make it up to God? There are plenty of suggestions for what we could do throughout the Bible and the history of the Church. Here's an early one.

> You shall take all the fat [of the bull] that covers the entrails, and the appendage of the liver, and the two kidneys with the fat that is on them, and turn them into smoke on the altar. But the flesh of the bull, and its skin, and its dung, you shall burn with fire outside the camp; it is a sin offering. (Exodus 29:13–14)

There are 130 references to sacrificing bulls or goats as sin offerings in the Old Testament, so that may be something to consider. (Anyone know where we can get a bull? And how many sins does one bull cover?) A more doable suggestion for our time would be this:

> When a man or a woman commits any sin against anyone else, thus breaking faith with the Lord, that person becomes guilty. Such persons will confess the sin they have done. Each will make payment for his guilt, add one-fifth more, and give it to the injured party. (Numbers 5:6–7)

We can confess, own up to our actions, admit our guilt, and pay restitution plus a penalty. Once the Church got organized, the plan of repeating the Lord's Prayer (and other prayers) and doing acts of goodness became acceptable ways of seeking God's forgiveness for sins committed. Of course, that practice opens up the question of, "How many 'Our Fathers' is enough?" How many acts of kindness make up for one terrible sin against a neighbor?

Oh, the questions that we worry about when we get

to worrying about sin: Is there a priority order of sins, from least to worst? How many times can I commit the same sin before I can forget about being forgiven? Does it matter if I planned to do the sin or if it was accidental? Is a sin against a neighbor worse than one against a stranger? What if I commit a sin that I am not aware of and die before I ask for forgiveness?

The remedy for sin is forgiveness. Forgiveness can be defined in many ways, but one quick way of explaining it is: Forgiveness is giving up my right, or desire, to hurt you for hurting me.

Forgiveness comes from God. Even the scribes of Jesus's day understood this: "Who can forgive sins but God alone?" (Mark 2:7). So, if forgiveness is a God thing how can we get in on it? How does God pass out forgiveness?

The foundational text for this chapter is Matthew 12:31, "Therefore, I tell you that people will be forgiven for every sin and insult to God. But insulting the Holy Spirit won't be forgiven."

Here's a question for you. Without writing anything down, how many times can you remember something happening before you lose count? For example, if I asked you to keep count of the number of days that it rained this year, could you tell me at the end of the year how many without having written anything down?

One day in Capernaum, Peter was listening to Jesus teach. Jesus said, "If your brother or sister sins against you, go and correct them when you are alone together. If they listen to you, [good] but if they don't, take a witness from the church and go try again ... but if they still don't ..."

The point Jesus was making was lost on Peter, because when Peter heard that you should try two or three times to forgive your brother or sister, his mind immediately went to, "How many times must I forgive and try to make things right?"

> Then Peter said, to Jesus, "Lord, how many times should I forgive my brother or sister who sins against me? Should I forgive as many as seven times? (Matthew 18:21)

Seven times? Perhaps that was as many times as Peter thought he could remember without writing anything down; remember, he had no iPad, not even a pencil and paper to make notes on. Or maybe he thought that because seven was a holy number, that ought to please God. Like most of us, Peter was willing to forgive—but up to a point. (There are limits after all, right?)

How do we decide to forgive? What conditions our willingness or ability to forgive? Let's have a show of hands; go ahead, no one is watching.

- Is it easier to forgive unintentional hurtful actions or intentional ones?
  - Is it easier to forgive sins against us that don't involve bodily injury, or ones that are physically painful?

- Is it easier to forgive family members? Friends? Strangers?
- Is it easier to forgive groups of people who are like us, or those who are not?

But what about God's forgiveness? What can we expect in the way of forgiveness from God? What criteria does God use to decide when to forgive? What do we have to do to be eligible to receive it? Are there restrictions or limitations? Do we get a certain number of chances before we strike out?

There are two ways of understanding how God's forgiveness works.

> If you forgive others their sins, your heavenly Father will also forgive you. But if you don't forgive others, neither will your Father forgive your sins. (Matthew 6:14–15)

The way most people hear that is that God's forgiveness is conditional on our willingness to forgive others: if we won't forgive others, God won't forgive us. The problem with that understanding is that it seems to imply that we have some control over God's decision to forgive or not to forgive. If I forgive, God forgives. If I don't forgive, God doesn't forgive. It's all in my hands. It makes God out to be like a child: "You did it first, so I am going to do it to you!" (More about this later.)

The other way of understanding God's forgiveness is drawn from the foundational text of today's lesson.

> I assure you that human beings will be forgiven for everything, *for all sins* and insults of every kind. But whoever insults the Holy Spirit will never be forgiven. That person is guilty of a sin with consequences that last forever. (Mark 3:28–29; emphasis added)

All human beings will be forgiven everything! That's quite a blanket statement. With the one exception of speaking against or denying the power of God's Holy Spirit, anything we do, and everything we might do, God forgives. Though this is the clearest statement of this promise, but this is not the first time we find it in the scriptures.

> When I bring clouds over the earth and the bow appears in the clouds, I will remember the covenant between me and you and every living being … Floodwaters will never again destroy all creatures. (Genesis 9:14–15)

After the flood, God made a covenant with Noah, his children, and "every living being" that he will never again act to destroy the earth. The rainbow in the sky is the reminder of God's promise to forgive the evil of humanity to this day! For God to make such a promise to love all of humanity who were to come after Noah indicates that

God does not intend to keep a running tab on all of our sins against him. If God were to count all our sins, that would leave open the possibility that at some point, God might grow weary of forgiving and think, "Enough is enough. I'm through forgiving them."

In Micah 7:18–19 we read,

> Who is a God like you, pardoning iniquity and overlooking the sin of your people? He doesn't hold on to his anger forever; he delights in faithful love. He will once again have compassion on us, he will tread down our iniquities. [He] will hurl all our sins into the depth of the sea.

In Matthew 1:21, the angel announces to the Virgin Mary,

> You will call him Jesus, because he will save his people from their sins.

Matthew 26:28 identifies the forgiveness of sins as the purpose of Jesus's sacrifice.

> Drink from this, all of you. This is my blood of the covenant, which is poured out for many so that their sins may be forgiven.

In 1 John 2:1–2 we read,

> My little children, I'm writing these things to you so that you don't sin. But if you do sin, we

have an advocate with the father, Jesus Christ the righteous one. He is God's way of dealing with our sins, not only ours but the sins of the whole world.

Remember Peter asking Jesus, "How many times must I forgive?" Jesus's answer to Peter was intended to guide Peter into a way of thinking about forgiveness much more in line with the way God forgives. God doesn't count how many times he has to forgive us. When Jesus said in our foundational text that "all sins will be forgiven," he was telling us that God doesn't forgive on a case-by-case basis, pondering each time, "Is this sin too bad? Is this too many times for that person?"

Through his eternal love, as expressed in the prophets and in the sacrifice of his Son, we know that God has already forgiven us whatever sins we have committed and will commit against him. God doesn't have to decide every time we do something whether or not he will forgive us. We live in God's eternal, constant, continuous forgiveness. God loves the world!

How can we forgive like that? Chances are we can't, but if we want to try, we need to understand how God's forgiveness differs from our own. It's a matter of direction. It's the difference between looking back and looking forward.

When we think of forgiving someone, our perspective is to look to the past and think about what that person did that hurt us and how many other times they have wronged us. Then we decide if we can bring ourselves to forgive their most recent sin. By looking to the past, we are remembering what was done and, in all likelihood, counting up how many times this person has wronged us until we, like Peter, ask ourselves, "How many times do I have to forgive him?" That's not the way God thinks.

God's perspective is not on the past but on what lies ahead. God decided before he formed the first ball of clay into the first person that no matter what, God was going to love his creatures, and that means forgiving us of whatever foolish or hurtful things we do.

> The Lord proclaims, "The people who survived … found grace in the wilderness. As Israel searched for a place to rest, the Lord appeared to them from a distance: I have loved you with a love that lasts forever. And so with unfailing love I have drawn you to myself." (Jeremiah 31:2)

> Give thanks to the Lord because he is good. God's faithful love lasts forever! (Psalm 136)

The author of that psalm was so intent on conveying that message that he repeats the truth that "God's faithful love lasts forever" twenty-six times in twenty-six verses! John makes the point that "God is love" (1 John 4:8). The psalmist's point is that God always loves! My take away is that God always only loves. And because love includes forgiveness, God always forgives.

This is how the love of God is revealed to us: God
has sent his only Son into the world so that we
can live through him. This is love: it is not that
we loved God but that he loved us and sent his
Son as the sacrifice that deals with our sins. Dear
friends, if God loved us this way, we also ought
to love each other. (1 John 4:10)

The message here is that you need not worry if
something you have done is forgivable or not, or what
you have to do to obtain God's forgiveness. The point
is you are already forgiven! You were forgiven before
you were born! Whatever you do is forgiven. God loves
you. and "love doesn't keep a record of complaints" (1
Corinthians 13:5b).

Love includes forgiveness. If God is love, then God
is 100 percent love, and 100 percent love includes 100
percent forgiveness.

When we covenant to love someone—a spouse, a
child, a friend—we are saying, "Whatever you do that
hurts me, I won't keep that hurt or anger because I have
made a covenant to love you. No matter what you do, you
are forgiven!"

It's a matter of looking forward, not back. "To have
and to hold from this day forward." No matter what
comes, be it for better or worse, richer or poorer, sickness
or health, I will love and cherish you! The only way God
could forgive the sins we haven't yet committed is because
God has made a covenant to love us no matter what
happens in the future.

So don't wonder whether you are forgiven or not. You are!

We have to focus on forgiving those who have sinned against us. Forgiveness brings the forgiver peace of mind and frees him or her from cancerous anger that spreads until it consumes us. Forgiveness involves letting go of deeply held negative feelings. It empowers us to recognize the pain we suffered without letting that pain control us. Forgiving enables us to heal and move on with our lives.

When Jesus said, "You can't be forgiven unless you forgive," he was saying that if your heart isn't open to forgiving others, it will not be open to receiving the forgiveness of God that is freely offered to you.

And that leads us right back to that one exception that we read about in the foundational text in Mark.

> I assure you that human beings will be forgiven for everything, for all sins and insults of every kind. But whoever insults the Holy Spirit will never be forgiven. That person is guilty of a sin with consequences that last forever. (Mark 3:28–29)

The older translations use the word *blasphemy* instead of *insult*, which is not a word in our daily vocabulary. It means "to revile, curse, slander, or despise someone." The meaning of Jesus's statement is that forgiveness will not be effectuated in the heart of someone who denies God. If God is offering you something, and you won't even acknowledge that God exists or that God has anything to offer that you could possibly want, then you willfully reject God's offer of forgiveness. That is the only possible unforgiveable sin. And even then it is not unforgiveable because forgiveness was not offered. It is unforgiveable because God's forgiveness <u>was</u> offered and rejected.

Of course, confessing our sins to God is a good and helpful thing. God doesn't need it—we do. To confess our sin is to acknowledge that God is to be worshipped and obeyed in our lives.

> If we confess our sins, he is faithful and just to forgive us our sins and cleanse us from everything we've done wrong. (1 John 1:9)

In addition to expressing our sincere regret for our hurtful actions, confessing is a most helpful way for us to take inventory of what we have done wrong and to consider how we might avoid making the same mistakes in the future.

> No one who conceals sins will prosper, but one who confesses [his sin] will obtain mercy. (Proverbs 28:13)

Like most of us parents, the Church has been guilty of saying things like, "If you do that again, God won't forgive you," "If you don't say you're sorry, God won't forgive you," "If you keep hurting people, God won't forgive you," and "God sees everything you do, and if God sees something he doesn't like, God won't forgive you."

We say things like that for the same reason the Church has long said things like that: to scare our children into good behavior. To intimidate people into obedience to God's holy will, for their own sakes.

I believe that foundational to grasping the message of the entire Bible, especially the New Testament Gospel, is hearing the promise of Jesus that it doesn't matter what sinful thing we have done—God forgives us. I think this is part of what Paul was telling the Romans when he said, "There is nothing that can separate us from God's love—nothing that can happen to us, and not anything we can do to harm ourselves, others, or the creation." (Romans 8:38-39)

The only requirement to activate that promise in our lives is our humbly acknowledging that we are not gods, that we are not the center of power, and that we need help getting through life without totally messing things up. We need the Father and know that God's way is the way that leads to abundant, joyful, eternal life.

> "Since the day we heard about you, we haven't stopped praying for you and asking for you to be filled with the knowledge of God's will, with all wisdom and spiritual understanding. We're praying this so that you can live lives that are worthy of the Lord and pleasing to him in every way: by producing fruit in every good work and growing in the knowledge of God; by being strengthened through his glorious might so that you endure everything and have patience; and by giving thanks with joy to the Father. He made it so you could take part in the inheritance, in

light granted to God's holy people. He rescued us from the control of darkness and transferred us into the kingdom of the Son he loves. He set us free through the Son and forgave our sins." (Colossians 1:9–14)

All our sins!

Chapter 9

When You Pray

Pray like this: Our Father …
—Matthew 6:9

THE BASIC ASPECT OF RELIGION is the understanding of what God is like and what is our relationship to God.

As long as there have been people, there has been religion. "Throughout history and beyond in the dark recesses of men's earliest cultures, religion has been a vital and pervasive feature of human life … Primitive peoples conceived of themselves as surrounded by a myriad of unseen forces" (Ninian Smart, *The Religious Experience of Mankind* Charles Scribner's Sons; New York; 1969;pages, 3, 29). Among those natural forces was what was called by various names "the life force." This was the force that caused life to come into being, assisted in sustaining life, and controlled whatever life there might be beyond this life. From the earliest times, there was a belief that some form of existence followed death.

We know this because of evidence found in ancient burial sites. Archeologists have documented graves with arrowheads and spear heads placed next to the hands of the deceased to provide weapons or tools for survival in whatever life is to follow death. In other locations, skeletons have been found that were bound up in the fetal position to prepare for a new birth into the next life.

Religion is the belief in and worship of a controlling power, especially a personal God or gods. Throughout the generations of humanity, the idea of what that controlling power was like passed through several iterations. But there has always been religion because humanity has always had an awareness that there must be something greater than itself, something that came before we did, and something that caused all things to come into being. Humanity has always had a sense that staying on the good side of that Great Something was to our advantage, so we have always sought to foster a good relationship with the Great Something.

Every relationship is built on communication in some form or another. When we make an attempt to communicate with the Great Something we want to be in relationship with, we call that prayer. Prayer is a form of worship. Prayer as worship has taken many forms throughout history—dance, music, sacrifice, posture, and speech, among others. How a tribe or congregation prays is a clear window on how they perceive their relationship with the Great Something to be structured.

In ancient Greece and Rome, prayers were made to whichever member of the pantheon of gods a farmer or merchant thought had authority over his crop or business. Because the gods were impersonal and may or may not have been listening, prayers generally began with a lengthy and flowery recounting of that particular god's heroic acts, great strengths, and mighty victories before getting around to one's prayerful plea. I suppose the idea was that a lot of flattery would gain the god's attention and appreciation.

Early on, the Hebrews also believed that there were many gods running around the cosmos, but their experiences had led them to believe that there was only one God who had final control over everything. That is called henotheism. The prayers of those early Hebrews (of which we have scant documentation) were offered to the God whom they perceived to have been Creator of all that is, Father of their tribes and nation, and Controller of the future. Though we have little record of what those personal prayers may have said, we do have the Book of Psalms. The Book of Psalms was the prayer book or song book of the Temple. The psalms take many forms— lament, petition, confession, praise—but are all prayers in one form or another.

The psalms were all written as poetry with no direct salutation at the beginning. However, within the first verse or two of most of the psalms, we find the name or title of the one who is being addressed, and that name or title is indicative of the perceived relationship between the one praying and the one being addressed.

As you quickly flip through the psalms, you will notice that most of them are addressed to either Lord or God (cf. Psalm 2, 3, 5, 8, 10, 16, 22, 25, 27, 35, 43, 44, 46, 54, 59, 60, and so on). *Lord*, like *King*, is an appellation for a person or deity who has total authority, control, or power over others, acting like a master, a chief, or a ruler.

Other sources relate that some of the Hebrew prayers were addressed to "Our Father and King" or "Father in Heaven," but it is significant to note that the use of "Father" was most likely in reference to God as the father of the nation, like our use of forefathers when referring to the founders of our country or others who have gone before. It was not reference to an emotional, personal relationship with God.

With the prayers of the Jews all addressed to their Lord or King, that tells us something about the way they perceived the relationship they had with the God they worshipped. God was the one who had power and control over them. God was the one of whom they should be afraid. God was the one who punished them for their mistakes. God was the one who could withhold bounty and blessing. God was the one whom they must appease.

Apparently in the time of Jesus, it was fashionable to be seen publicly praying loudly while employing elaborate phrases to show just how pious you were, and to draw a crowd to impress when you dropped your offering into the box. It was a point of pride to have people standing near and whispering about you: "He must be really loved by God because he could go on praying for an hour at a time and was never at a loss for big words!" This is what Jesus said about that.

When you pray, don't be like the hypocrites. They love to pray standing in the synagogues and on the street corners so that people will see them. I assure you, that's the only reward they'll get. But when you pray, go to your room, shut the door, and pray to your Father who is present in that secret place. Your Father who sees what you do in secret will reward you.

When you pray, don't pour out a flood of empty words, as the Gentiles do. They think that by saying many words they'll be heard. Don't be like them, because your Father knows what you need before you ask.

When you pray, pray like this: Our Father ... (Matthew 6:5–8)

One day, his friends asked Jesus to teach them how to pray, so he did. He said you don't need to be so formal as to address God as Lord or King; you can just call him Father. From many of his other words, we know that Jesus was not thinking of God as a forefather but as a personal, loving, compassionate father, and we should do the same (cf. Matthew 10:29, 18:13–14; Luke 6:36, 11:13, 15:20; John 3:35).

The word Jesus used for *Father* was not the formal *pater*, indicating the patriarch, but the informal, childlike word *abba*. *Abba*, like *Dada* or *Momma*, is one of the first sounds a child is likely to make and compares to *Daddy* or *Mommy* in our time. It is an intimate term.

Therefore when we pray the way Jesus taught us to

pray, we are not addressing some distant Lord who is holding power and control over us, waiting to punish our smallest mistakes. We are addressing one who is with us in our secret places. One who is looking to bring us back from the dangers we wander into. One who is compassionate and longs to hold us in his arms like the shepherd who cradles the lost sheep that is found. One who gives his children all good things. That is foundational.

These words are foundational because they are so basic, so revolutionary to our understanding of the God of the whole Bible. To be given permission to call God "Father" changes everything in our relationship with the Great Something!

Let's take a quick look at the prayer that follows.

"Hallowed be thy name" or "Holy is your name"

When praying this phrase, I am declaring that the name of God is held by me to be all I need. God's name is not just some inconsequential name that is easily forgettable. In God is wholeness, completeness, health, and peace. I call upon the holy name of God because from the One who is whole, I can learn about and will be led in the ways of goodness.

"May your kingdom come, and your will be done on earth as it is in heaven"

To pray for the kingdom of God to come and for God's will to be done is both a prayer of hope and a personal commitment to join the movement to make that happen. In putting this phrase in the prayer, Jesus was saying to us, "Don't give up on God. Abraham was one hundred years old and still waiting for the first of what was promised to be a multitude of babies! Continue to have hope."

The kingdom of God will surely be a situation where all of God's precious children will live freely and in peace and have access to all they need for abundant and joyful lives. Surely the will of God that we pray for in the Lord's Prayer is for all children to grow up with possibilities and promise and that all the sick will be cared for and all the strangers will be welcomed, fed, clothed, and sheltered. But how will that happen without our involvement? How will the kingdoms of this world be brought to their knees until those who have glimpsed the kingdom of God in the life of Jesus organize and march against the lies of self-preservation and personal greed?

"Give us the bread we need for today"

This is not a request for a sandwich in our lunch box every day. This is an out and out confession of trust in God to provide. The people who heard Jesus say "daily bread" thought immediately back to the daily manna from God that sustained their ancestors for forty years in the wilderness.

They also remembered that the daily manna came with a caveat. "Remember," they were told, "only collect enough for one day, just enough for the family. Except on the weekends when you can collect enough for Saturday and Sunday as well. And don't try to horde it away for fear that there won't be any tomorrow. There will be more tomorrow!" (Exodus 16).

That caveat was saying, "Trust me," says the Lord your God. "Trust me to take care of you every day." And through all those years of wilderness camping, God did take care of them, never missing a day. So when Jesus said to ask God for daily bread, he was telling us to trust God. Asking for just enough for each day and no more is a way of declaring our trust in God for tomorrow and all the days after that.

"Forgive us for the ways we have wronged you, just as we also forgive those who have wronged us"

Jesus could have left it at "forgive us," but he didn't. He added "just as." Just as we forgive those who have wronged us, meaning, "to the same extent or degree that we forgive others," or, "in the same manner as we forgive others."

> "Father, forgive us with the same eagerness or hesitancy that we forgive others."
> "Father, forgive us with the same willingness or reluctance that we forgive others."
> "Father, forgive us with the same swiftness or delay that we forgive others."

"Father, forgive us with the same sincerity or
insincerity that we forgive others."

Jesus wasn't just telling us that we have the right to
expect God to forgive us only if we forgive others, or when
we forgive others, but in the same way that we forgive
others. If we are going to keep praying, "Father, forgive
me just as I forgive others," we should remind ourselves
that what we are really saying is, "Father, treat me the way
I intend to treat those who have done me wrong, those
who owe me something, and those at whom I am really
angry!"

"And lead us not into temptation, but deliver us from evil"

Remember that other foundational text that said,
"God is good all the time"? If God were to lead us into
temptation and not deliver us from evil, that would not be
good. The meaning of this phrase is a plea for God to lead
us out of, or away from, the temptations that surround us
and threaten us.

Recently, Pope Francis approved changes to the
wording of this phrase in the prayer. Instead of saying,
"Lead us not into temptation," Catholics will now say, "Do
not let us fall into temptation." The pope said he thought
the English translation of the prayer at that point was not
correct. "It is not a good translation because it speaks of a
God who induces temptation. I am the one who falls. It's
not him pushing me into temptation to then see how I have
fallen. A father doesn't do that; a father helps you to get

up immediately. It's Satan who leads us into temptation; that's his department." (CBNNEWS.com, June 4, 2019)

Try hearing it this way: "God, I will follow you wherever you lead me, but if we get too close to something really tempting, remember that I am weak. I can't promise that I won't give in to that temptation. If I do, please deliver me from whatever evil of my own making that may result."

What we should not hear Jesus saying is that God might just lead us toward some temptations that we won't be able to withstand as some sort of callous test to see how faithful we really are. Nor should we think that in a moment of distraction over something more important than what we are facing, our loving, heavenly Father would allow evil to consume us—like setting us down next to a fire and forgetting about us until the fire overtakes us!

Jesus is instructing us to rely on the Father's leading to keep us going along the paths of righteousness, where we will be safe from temptation and the reach of evil, or the "evil one."

"For Thine is the kingdom, and the power, and the glory forever. Amen"

Obviously, this doxology is not included in Matthew or Luke at the end of the prayer that Jesus gave. But it is scriptural.

The various manuscripts of Matthew's gospel that still exist contain ten different endings for the Lord's Prayer.

The oldest, and those considered to be the best, do not include this final doxology. Most of the later copies of the book include these words. This is considered indication of the widespread use of these words as an act of worship by the early Church, either publicly or privately. But where do they come from?

At the end of 1 Chronicles, the last act of King David was to gather all of Israel and announce that all of his estate, his wealth, and that of the government was being signed over for the construction of the temple that he had not been allowed to build but that his son Solomon would build. He then told the elders to get out their checkbooks and be generous (1 Chronicles 29:1–9). Then as the celebration was drawing to a close, David blessed the Lord in the presence of the people and said,

> Yours, O Lord, are the greatness, the power, the glory, the victory, and the majesty; for all that is in the heavens and on the earth is yours; yours is the kingdom, O Lord, and you are exalted as head above it … In your hand are power and might; and it is in your hand to make great and to give strength to all. And now, our God, we give thanks to you and praise your glorious name. (1 Chronicles 29:11–13 NRSV)

One last word. (Actually, it was the first word).

"Our"

Before Jesus teaches us anything else about prayer, he teaches us to begin with the inclusive word *our*.

In all likelihood, when the people listening to Jesus on the hillside that afternoon in Galilee heard Jesus begin praying by saying, "Our Father," they were sure he meant "the Father of our own people," our kind, our kin, those who are like us and worship the same way we do and believe the same way we do.

But that is not what Jesus meant, is it?

How do we know? We are talking about the same Jesus who told the story of a despised Samaritan who stopped to help when "our own kind" just passed by. We are talking about the Jesus who healed the Gentile servant of an enemy soldier. We are talking about the Jesus who commissioned us to "go into all the world," to go beyond our own land, to go to people of all races and nations because "God so loves the world," and to bring people of all kinds into his all-inclusive community.

"Our Father!" Jesus clearly wanted us to begin our prayers with the reminder that the Father who is in heaven is the Father of all people, because the love of God excludes no one! God is your Father, whoever you are, and God is my Father. And that is foundational to a clear understanding the entire Bible.

Chapter 10

A Great Paradox

Love your enemies.
—Matthew 5:44

THE BIBLE IS FULL OF paradoxes, such as 1 Samuel 2:6–8, Ezekiel 21:26, Matthew 23:11, Mark 9:35, Luke 17:33, and James 1:2.

A paradox is a statement that makes no sense but is true. For example, "Whoever wants to be greatest among you should be everyone's servant" (Matthew 23:11), or "Anyone who wants to be first, must be the very least" (Mark 9:35), or "When I'm weak, then I'm strong" (2 Corinthians 12:10).

The only way those things can be true is if the way things seem to be is not the reality of the way things are. Take greatness. In my trusty dictionary, greatness is defined using such words as "powerful, influential, eminent, and distinguished." In today's vernacular people who are great are celebrities, athletes, the super wealthy, and world leaders because everyone knows them, wants to be them, and pays to see their movies or read their books. Greatness seems to be the ability to attract attention and a big payoff.

So, how can a servant be called great? A servant performs humble services. A servant is submissive to the needs of an employer. A servant stays in the background and tries to go unnoticed. A servant is underpaid, if paid at all. How can a servant be considered great? In this world, that makes no sense; that's simply not the way things are. Paul said it this way:

> Do not be conformed to this world, but be transformed by the renewing of your minds, so that you may discern what is the will of God—what is good and acceptable and perfect. (Romans 12:2)

The reality of the way things are is that there are two kingdoms. There is the kingdom controlled by human desire, and there is that other kingdom controlled by the will of God. Jesus invites those who follow him to "seek first the kingdom of God" and not worry about what's in your closet or your pantry, or what your Facebook "friends" are saying about you.

Once we are living in God's kingdom, it no longer matters who may be against us, because God is for us! In God's kingdom, the ones who are great are the ones who are most like God, and God did not withhold even his only Son, but gave him up to serve all of us

(Romans 8:31–39). That makes the servant great in God's kingdom.

Do you want to be great?

> Adopt the attitude that was in Christ Jesus: Though he was in the form of God, he did not consider being equal with God something to exploit. But he emptied himself by taking the form of a servant and by becoming like human beings. When he found himself in the form of a human, he humbled himself becoming obedient to the point of death, even death on a cross. Therefore, God highly honored him [made him great] and gave him a name above all names [made him famous] so that at the name of Jesus everyone in heaven and on earth, and under the earth might bow and every tongue confess that Jesus Christ is Lord, to the glory of God the Father [and greater than a gazillion YouTube hits!]. (Philippians 2:5–11)

There is an old hymn by George Matheson in which every line is a paradox.

> Make me a captive, Lord, and then I shall be free,
> Force me to render up my sword,
> and I shall conqueror be.
> I sink in life's alarms when by myself I stand;
> Imprison me within thine arms, and
> strong shall be my hand.

My heart is weak and poor until it master find,
It has no spring of action sure, it varies with the wind.
It cannot freely move till thou hast wrought its chain;
Enslave it with thy matchless love
and deathless it shall reign.

My power is faint and low till I have learned to serve,
It lacks the needed fire to glow, it
lacks the breeze to nerve.
It cannot drive the world until itself be driven;
Its flag can only be unfurled when
thou shalt breathe from heaven.

My will is not my own till thou hast made it thine,
If it would reach a monarch's throne,
it must its crown resign.
It only stands unbent amid the clashing strife
When on thy bosom it has leant,
and found in thee its life.
("The United Methodist Hymnal; United Methodist
Publishing House; Nashville; 1999; page 421)

There is one other paradox I want to lift up, and it
is this one that I am naming as the foundational text for
this chapter.

> You have heard it said, "You must love your
> neighbor and hate your enemy." But I say to you,
> love your enemies and pray for those who harass
> you. (Matthew 5:43–44)

How many remember those "duck and cover" drills from the early 1950s? (If you don't, ask Grandma and Grandpa.) I remember being told that when we heard the siren, we should all get down and crawl under our desks to protect us from the blast and fallout. We knew about the mean Russians, who wanted to take over our country and were planning to launch atomic bombs at us. We knew the threat was real and felt it in our deepest selves.

The problem for me was that our school (in Miami) was built before there was any idea of air-conditioned schools. That meant that one wall of each classroom was built with windows from floor to ceiling. As I was crouching under my desk during one of the drills, I looked out the windows, scanned the sky for those incoming Russian bombers, and thought, "What about all that glass? When the bomb blast hits, all those windows are going to rain down shards of glass on all of us! We are all going to die!"

That's how I remember "duck and cover" drills, thinking, "This is ridiculous. This wooden desk is not going to save any of us from a blast of flying glass!"

I also remember hearing about the Doomsday Clock which counted the time remaining until the world was going to be consumed by some man-made castrophe. At first I had a hard time understanding that when they said the Doomsday Clock was just "two minutes until midnight," they were talking metaphorically and not literally!

Later, there were phrases like "mutually assured destruction," "nuclear winter" and "doomsday scenario."

There was SALT (Strategic Arms Limitation Treaty) and START (Strategic Arms Reduction Treaty). Much later we all remember learning that WMD meant "weapons of mass destruction."

My grandchildren were issued ankle identification bands to wear at school in case of a mass destruction event. That Doomsday Clock keeps on ticking in the back of the minds of those of us who actually ducked and covered in front of glass walls that would do nothing but give us one last brief glimpse of the incoming bombs.

However, nuclear warheads weren't the first weapons of mass destruction the world has known. Two thousand years ago, the WMD had another name: Rome.

Rome had the power to blanket a smaller kingdom with enough troops to totally destroy its crops and livestock, wipe out its population, consume or destroy its resources, and remove its memory from history. Rome was a weapon of mass destruction, and because of her lust for power and security and territory, Rome was the enemy of the world!

The world has, for a long time, been in a constant search for peace. The most feared weapons the world has ever known were all created as means to bring about peace. Peace is essential for humanity to thrive. Without peace, the destructive nature of our species will continue to drive us toward mutual destruction.

In an article titled *Peace Builds, Strengthens and Restores*, Rev. Kent Winters-Hazelton writes,

> Peace is the desire of every beating heart. Peace is the hope of every nation, the promise of every

politician, the pulse of every religious tradition, the goal of every prayer. Peace is the bold, courageous and ultimate response to the [false] notion that violence provides any viable solution for the conflicts of our world. Where war destroys and tears apart, peace builds, strengthens and restores. At the same time peace is personal, for each of us longs for security and tranquility in the face of the troubles, anxiety and chaos that often touch our lives. (Faith Forum: Why is peace important? Saturday, July 17, 2010)

Our loving, always present, and all-knowing God has not left us without an answer to our questions about how to find peace and remove the fears of war and destruction at the hands of our enemies. On a "silent night" long ago, the angelic messengers of God broke through the boundaries of heaven and proclaimed, "Glory to God in heaven, and on earth, peace."

The purpose of the whole Christ event, the incarnation of God on earth, was to bring an answer to the question of how the world can ever find peace in the presence of our enemies. The answer, as Jesus gave it, is at once so simple and yet not so simple at all. It is the great paradox!

The writer of Matthew has highlighted the Sermon on the Mount as the first and greatest teaching event of Jesus's ministry. It is a sermon about how to get along with the other people we are forced to deal with every day. It is a lesson about ethics and morality, about how to live together in community peacefully. Selecting one verse from that sermon as a "foundational text" over so many other important, inspiring, challenging, and cherished texts was a daunting task because all of the words of Jesus are of ultimate value for the hearer.

In searching for that foundational text in the sermon, I was looking for something that stood out, something that was unique to Jesus, something that was not a repetition of what had been said before by others, and something that is not found in other faith expressions (as far as I know). Matthew 5:44 jumped out.

> But I say to you, love your enemies and pray for those who harass you.

Now that is a paradox! Enemies are precisely those people whom we don't love! Enemies are those people who are actively out to hurt us. An enemy is one who is being hostile toward us.

> In the Old Testament most of the references to enemies are to national enemies. The Hebrew word used is often translated as "adversary" or "foe." Its literal meaning is to surround, encircle, to tie up, to envelop, to hamper, to cramp. (*The New Interpreters Dictionary of the Bible*, vol. 2, 259)

An enemy is a person who is surrounding you, who is trying to tie you up, and who is actively engaged in harming you. I think at times when we hear this paradoxical command from Jesus, we tend to think about something less than that. When Jesus says, "Love your enemies," we think of a neighbor we don't get along with, a family member we can't tolerate, a coworker we don't trust, or the guy who stole our parking space. (As if there actually was a parking space with our name on it!)

The truth is, those people come under the category of neighbors—good neighbors, bad neighbors, likeable and unlikeable neighbors, familiar neighbors and stranger neighbors, friendly neighbors and irritating neighbors. Jesus tells us to love our neighbors, no question. To love them as we love ourselves. To love them as God loves us. When Jesus told us to love our neighbors, as he repeatedly did in the gospels, he was quoting from the Old Testament. He was reminding the people what they already knew God wanted them to do.

> You must not act unjustly in a legal case. Do not show favoritism to the poor or deference to the great; you must judge your fellow Israelites fairly. Do not go around slandering your people. Do not stand by while your neighbor's blood is shed. I am the Lord. You must not hate your fellow Israelite in your heart. Rebuke your fellow Israelite strongly … but do not take revenge nor hold a grudge against any of your own people. Instead, you must love your neighbor as yourself. I am the Lord. (Leviticus 19:15–18)

The implication in Leviticus is clear. The obligation

to love your neighbor is limited to those of your own people, to fellow Israelites—not to those who are from outside the community. One of the difficulties I have with the Old Testament theology is the interpretation that because God chose the line and family of Abraham to be his chosen people, they were showing loyalty to God by keeping that bloodline pure by not intermarrying with outsiders. One way to make sure that didn't happen was to isolate themselves from outsiders, even to the point of considering outsiders a danger and their enemies.

The great tension that existed between the Jews and the Samaritans in Jesus's day came from the time when the exiles were returned from Babylon and began to rebuild the city and the temple. The folks from Samaria offered to help, but the Judeans rejected that help because the Jews from the north had intermarried with people from other captured nations. They had blended their blood with foreigners and were therefore not considered "pure." The enemy were those not like us.

To the people of Jesus's day, it was very clear that the enemy was not only the Samaritans but the dominating world power, Rome. They were very familiar with the command to "love their neighbors" but found it a difficult and distasteful injunction where those two groups were concerned. They were even trying to come up with a narrow definition of "Who is my neighbor?" so they wouldn't really have to love all those other impure people.

When Jesus said, "Love your neighbor," I'm sure they all grumbled and said, "Yeah, yeah, we know that's what we should do. We are trying."

But when Jesus said, "You have heard it said that you must love your neighbor and hate your enemy. But I say to you love your enemy and pray for those who hurt you so that you will be acting as children of your Father who is in heaven," they must have looked around and said, "What? What did he say? Did anyone else hear that? Love the Romans? Is he kidding?"

No, he wasn't kidding. Remember those "duck and cover" drills, the Doomsday Clock, and the world longing for peace? How can we get past the fear of war and annihilation? How can the world change course and become less terrified and defensive? How can we make this a more peaceful planet?

> As Jesus came to the city and observed it, he wept over it. He said, "If only you knew on this of all days the things that lead to peace. But now they are hidden from your eyes. The time will come when your enemies will build fortifications around you, encircle you, and attack you from all sides. They will crush you completely, you and the people within you. They won't leave one stone on top of another within you, because you didn't recognize the time of your gracious visit from God." (Luke 9:41–44)

The things that make for peace—what might those things be? Spying on the enemy? Retaliation against the enemy? Building better weapon systems than the enemy has? Preemptive attacks? Invading and conquering foreign lands? Isolating and guarding borders from invasion? Truth is, we've tried all those things to no avail. So what would be the risks of loving our enemies on a personal or national scale?

In the upper room, with a room full of worried disciples who were consumed with the fear of what would happen to them after Jesus was no longer with them, Jesus said,

> Do not be afraid, let not your hearts be troubled. I will not leave you alone. My peace I leave with you. My peace is not like the peace of Rome [(the Pax Romana)] which is peace only as long as you do what your enemy commands you to do. My peace is the peace of knowing that nothing your enemy can do to you can remove you from the love of the Father. (John 14:27)

Jesus's command to "love your enemy" was as startling and absurd sounding to them as it is to us. Enemies are, by definition, those people whom we don't love! But if peace is what we really want, and not just a temporary triumph or victory over our foes, then active, assertive love is the way it is going to happen. The longer we do things that make others think of us as their enemy, the longer it will be before peace really does have a chance.

If the nations of the world perceive us as those who are surrounding them, hemming them in on all sides, treating them as our food or fuel suppliers, and using them to enlarge our storehouses as takers and not givers, then we have made ourselves the enemy of nations, and the lack of peace is our fault.

Loving their enemies is something that people and nations have seldom done with any great conviction or success. But that is what will make for peace. As long as enemies are not loved, peace will not be realized. What can we do? How can we begin to love our enemies?

- We can begin by praying for them—not praying for their downfall but praying for good things to be poured out upon them.
- We can teach our children to accept and appreciate the beautiful differences in peoples and cultures.
- We can treat people fairly, with justice, and not from an "I am better than you" starting point.

Actually, Paul very clearly spells out what must be done to live at peace with our enemies in his letter to the church that was sitting right in the heart of enemy territory: Rome.

Love should be shown without pretending. Hate evil, and hold on to what is good. Love each other like the members of your family. Be the best at showing honor to each other. Don't hesitate to be enthusiastic—be on fire in the Spirit as you serve the Lord! Be happy in your hope, stand your ground when you're in trouble, and devote yourselves to prayer. Contribute to the needs of God's people, and welcome strangers into your home. Bless people who harass you—bless and don't curse them. Be happy with those who are happy, and cry with those who are crying. Consider everyone as equal, and don't think that you're better than anyone else. Instead, associate with people who have no status. Don't think that you're so smart. Don't pay back anyone for their evil actions with evil actions, but show respect for what everyone else believes is good.

If possible, to the best of your ability, live at peace with all people. Don't try to get revenge for yourselves, my dear friends, but leave room for God's wrath. It is written, "Revenge belongs to me; I will pay it back," says the Lord. Instead, if your enemy is hungry, feed him; if he is thirsty, give him a drink. By doing this, you will pile burning coals of fire upon his head. Don't be defeated by evil, but defeat evil with good. (Romans 12:9–21)

"Love your enemies." Sounds crazy. It's a hard command to hear. It makes us uncomfortable, and we don't want to do it. But if we want peace, that is the way. And we surely do have to find a way to "turn this world upside down."

Prayer for Peace

Remember, Prince of Peace, the peoples of
the world divided into many nations
and tongues. Deliver us from every evil that
obstructs your saving purpose, and fulfill
your promises of old to establish your kingdom of peace.
From the curse of war and all that
creates it, O Lord, deliver us.
From believing and speaking lies against other nations,
from narrow loyalties and selfish
isolation, O Lord, deliver us.
From fear and distrust of other nations,
from all false pride, vainglory, and self-
conceit, O Lord, deliver us.
From the lust of the mighty for riches,
that drives peaceful people to
slaughter, O Lord, deliver us.
From putting our trust in the weapons of war,
and from lack of faith in the power of justice
and good will, O Lord, deliver us.
From every thought, word, and deed
which separates us from the perfect
realization of your love, O Lord, deliver us.
Amen.
(The United Methodist Book of
Worship;1992; page 520)

Chapter 11

God Loves

God so loved the world that he gave his only Son.
—John 3:16

It had been a difficult few days for Jesus. He had attended a wedding with his mother up north in Cana, and it was now time for the Passover feast. He traveled (walked!) the ninety or so miles down to Jerusalem. When he got to the temple, I imagine he was hoping for some quiet meditation time. What he found was the crazy, cacophonous confusion of the crowded market stalls in the temple courtyard.

When he saw what was happening, it is not too overstated to say that he lost it! His normally patient demeanor was overextended, and he couldn't close his eyes to what he was seeing. He grabbed a length of rope, made a whip out of it, and began going after those who were selling animals for the sacrifices, spices and vegetables for the meals, as well as the money changers who were always known to be unfair in how they determined their exchange rates, but now they were just out-and-out price-gouging the travelers who had come to the festival.

It didn't take long for the temple authorities to move in on him. It's a wonder they didn't arrest him on the spot! But they quickly began interrogating him. "Show us your ID. Tell us by what authority are you doing these things. And your answer had better be really good— miraculous, even!"

Jesus held his ground and said something his attackers didn't understand: "Destroy this temple and in three days I will raise it up." (John 2:19) Thinking he was talking about the temple of stone and wood behind them, they laughed at him. But the temple Jesus was talking about was his body. "After he was raised from the dead, his disciples remembered what he had said, and they believed the scripture and the words that Jesus had spoken." (John 2:21-22) The whole time Jesus was in Jerusalem during the festival, people were surrounding him. Many became believers after listening to him and seeing the miraculous signs that he did.

I'm sure he was tired and wanted nothing more than a peaceful night's sleep. But during the night, a couple of his disciples shook him awake and said that there was a guy outside asking to speak to him. One of the Jewish leaders, a Pharisee, had come to see him. I'm sure Jesus recognized him as one of the cluster of Pharisees and lawyers who were always listening from the back of the crowd, but he may not have known his name.

The man introduced himself as Nicodemus and

proceeded to make a startling statement to Jesus. "We know that you are a teacher who has come from God, for no one could do these miraculous signs that you do unless God is with him." (John 3:1) Whether he was speaking on behalf of a group of the Pharisees or just for himself, we do not know, but it didn't matter. He was the only one brave enough to risk coming at night to meet with the man the rest of them were trying to silence. Jesus didn't acknowledge the flattery; rather, he got straight to the question that he perceived was on Nicodemus' mind: "What do I have to do to follow you?"

"You have to start over, Nicodemus. You have to be born over again—you need a new starting point, a new beginning. You were born into this physical life through your mother's body. Now you need a new spiritual life. You have to start all over again, understanding that God wants more from you than for you to just keep all the old laws. God wants you to know that he loves you even when you forget a law, and God wants you to love your neighbors rather than judging them for each infraction of the law they may be guilty of."

After a brief discussion, Jesus said to him,

> Moses lifted up the snake in the wilderness [to display the power and presence of God] so must the Son of Man be lifted up so that everyone [will see in him the power and presence of God] and everyone who believes in him will have eternal life. [The truth is, Nicodemus, that] God loved the world so much that he gave his only Son, so

that no one who believes in him will perish but will have eternal life. God didn't send his Son into the world to judge the world, but that the world might be saved through him. Whoever believes in him isn't judged; whoever doesn't believe in him is already judged [by their own rejection of God's love as displayed in God's only Son]. (John 3:14–18)

There it is, today's foundational text: "God loved the world so much that he gave his only Son—not to judge or condemn the world, but so that the world might be saved" — saved from its own foolishness and selfishness and anger and hatred. Those are not the things that God wants for the world, and sending his only Son is the extent God was willing to go to save us from our sin.

Let's break that down. I started with the story of Nicodemus because even though John 3:16 is perhaps the most beloved verse in the Bible, it was addressed to a single person who had a deep sense of his own guilt and a longing to know what he had to do to get right with God. As this verse is addressed to his condition, so it speaks to ours.

"God loved the world"

Actually, God loves the world. This is not just an old story—this is contemporary. This is a message for us today, and we need to hear it today just as much as Nicodemus needed to hear it.

Our world is filled with violence. Often that violence against others is excused as security or protection against what others may do or have done to us, be it preemptive war against national enemies, street violence against a rival gang, or road rage against a perfect stranger. And there is violence generated by hatred and anger: domestic violence, racial violence, and violence against anyone who is different in religion or lifestyle from us.

Selfishness also permeates our world. What do I want? What will make me feel good? What is best for me? What is best for us against them? Trickle-down security, or, making sure I have what I need to be safe, well-fed, and comfortable before looking out for the needs of others, is not "loving our neighbors the way Jesus loved us." Self-centeredness that says, "I am not going to wear a mask whether it endangers others or not," is not "doing unto others as we would have them do to us." Selfishness that wants to purchase bananas or clothing at such low prices that those who harvest them and the children who stich them cannot be paid a livable wage is not serving the "least among us" the way Christ calls us to do.

We have fouled the rivers and streams with our trash. We have polluted the air with our industrial waste. We have hunted beautiful animals to extinction and destroyed the habitats of others with no regard for their benefit to ecosystems, or to our very existence.

But God still loves the world. Knowing that God loves this world is foundational to truly understanding the rest of the Bible, especially those parts that seem to say that God is angry with or ready to give up on the world and is preparing to destroy this world and everything in it. God is in love with the world and is committed to staying with the world and leading us to better practices, better attitudes, and better relationships.

"So much that he gave"

God gives. God doesn't barter or negotiate. God doesn't charge a price. God doesn't work a deal. God doesn't trade for something else. God gives and demands nothing in return. God gives to everyone. "God makes his sun to rise on the just and the unjust. God makes his rain to fall on the righteous and the unrighteous alike" (Matthew 5:45).

> Why should I fear in times of trouble, when the iniquity of my persecutors surrounds me, those who trust their wealth and boast of the abundance of their riches? Truly, no ransom [is enough] for one's life, there is no price one can give to God for it. For the ransom for life is costly, and can never be enough that one should live on forever and never see the grave. (Psalm 49:5–9)

God loves the world, and God gives freely to the world. What does God give?

"God gave his only Son"

In days gone by, a man's firstborn son was his most highly prized possession. A man's son was his legacy, his immortality, in the sense that his son would continue his name and reputation. A man's son would pass on the stories of his life and would be the representation of all that the man stood for.

Remembering that Jesus was talking to a man (Nicodemus), Jesus used a metaphor that spoke to that man's understanding. God gave his Son, and not only a Son but his only Son. Nicodemus well understood the concept that when you see a man's son, you see the man. A man's son is his reflection. What you get from the son comes from the father. When a father gives his son, he is giving himself.

> No one comes to the Father except through me. If you have really known me, you will also know the Father. From now on you know him and have seen him … Whoever has seen me has seen the Father … I am in the Father and the Father is in me. (John 14:6–9)

By understanding that metaphor, we can clearly say that in giving the Son, God has given himself to the world that he loves. God has held nothing back. God is in the Son just as the Son is from the Father.

In his opening words, the writer of the Gospel of John expressed it this way:

> In the beginning was the Word and the Word was with God and the Word was God. The Word was with God in the beginning … The Word became

flesh and dwelt among us (Jesus). We have seen his glory, glory like that of a father's only son, full of grace and truth. (John 1:1–4)

That is why we call him Immanuel (which means "God is with us"), because he is truly God with us, God among us, and God like us so he could show us and tell us what God is like.

"So that everyone who believes in him won't perish"

"It is not the will of our Heavenly Father that even one of his little ones should perish"—should be lost to their own destructive nature, should suffer from their own stupidity or foolishness, or should ever live separated from the Father's love. What God wants is for all of us to have eternal life—life beyond the grave.

"God didn't send his Son to judge the world"

If our sins were to be judged by some heavenly standard of justice, held up to the example of how God loves and forgives and gives so freely, we would never stand a chance for any hope of a reduced punishment! We would all be guilty as hell!

"But that the world might be saved through him"

Saved from what? Saved from destroying ourselves. Saved from the results of our hatred and anger and violence and greed. Saved from an eternity of separation from the love of the One who wants always to love us.

The word that stands out to me in that phrase is *might*. *Might* implies that there is no guarantee that being saved from deserved punishment for our sin will happen. But when we read the verse that promises that all sins are forgiven (Mark 3:28), we learn there is only one way that we could miss out on the promise of salvation and eternal life with the Father, and that way is for us to say, "No, thank you," and turn our backs on the gift of forgiving love that is offered to us and to the world through Jesus Christ.

> Whoever believes in him isn't judged; whoever doesn't believe in him is already judged, because they don't believe in the name of God's only Son. (John 3:18)

There is a difficulty with this part of the text. The problem is that for a long time, the Church understood this to say that anyone who didn't pronounce the name "Jesus" didn't believe in him. It didn't matter whether people had ever even heard the name spoken. The only way to heaven, the Church taught, was to say the name "Jesus" in your prayers.

The phrase "in the name of" can be understood in more than one way. It can mean a literal acceptance that one named Jesus lived. I believe that. Or it can mean "I believe in all that that person named Jesus taught. I believe in Jesus. I think his ways were right, and I am going to follow him. I'm going to live in the name of Jesus."

But what about the person who loves his neighbor, does good to those who abuse him, and gives thanks to the Creator by trying to take care of the creation—but that person has never heard the stories about the one who was named Jesus because we, the Church, haven't completed our mission of "going into all the world" with the gospel?

And what about the one who was abused by a priest or rejected by the Church because of her sexuality? As a result, she rejects organized religion and doesn't want to hear stories about the One the Church represents, but she still loves her neighbor and forgives, does good to any who abuse her, and gives thanks to the Creator by trying to take care of the creation. She feeds the poor and cares for the sick. What about that one? Is she turned away from heaven because of the scars on her life that make her angry at the Jesus the Church has misrepresented to her?

What about those who pray facing Mecca, or those who light menorahs at Hanukah, or the ones who follow the paths of the Buddha, yet they still love their neighbors, do good to those who abuse them, and give thanks to the Creator by trying to take care of the creation, feed the poor, and care for the sick? What about them? Will the God who loved the world—the whole world—so much that he came in our form to tell us of that love reject them because the name Jesus is not in their vocabulary?

To me, that would negate all that was said in the other foundational texts that we have studied: that God is with us always, that God hears the cries of his children, that God is our shepherd and tenderly cares for us, that God forgives the sins of the whole world, and that the least stand a chance to become the greatest in God's kingdom.

In John 10:16, we find words that may seem somewhat obscure at first.

> I am the good shepherd. I know my own sheep and they know me, just as the Father knows me and I know the Father. I give up my life for the sheep. I have other sheep that don't belong to this fold. I must lead them too. They will listen to my voice and there will be one flock, with one shepherd.

Who are Christ's "other sheep"? I think Jesus was referring to people who are not necessarily of the Christian flock but who nonetheless listen to his voice calling them to love one another and to do good to others, just as he tells us to do.

That God loves the world seems so basic and obvious to us because we have been privileged to have heard that since our birth. But there are those who still live in the darkness of doubting that there is any good in this world and no hope that anything will ever get any better. They live in fear of whatever angry forces control the days and cause the storms to sweep over us. Someone needs to tell them that there is a good and loving God who holds the whole world in his hands!

Being taught that God loves the world and then going

out into that world and finding evidence of that love is truly a gift of redeeming grace. We find that evidence in the freshness of spring, in the joy of children, in the sacrifices being made by doctors and nurses treating the sick, in the acceptance offered to me by those who are different from me, and in all the other ways and places that the face of God shines through the gloom and despair. That is a gift that makes life joyful and abundant and worth the living! That is the gift the church has to give to the world.

"God so loved the world that he gave his only Son, that whosoever believes in him shall not perish but have everlasting life"—a life not judged but justified, not condemned but saved. That really is foundational! Thanks be to God.

"And Can It Be"
by Charles Wesley

And can it be that I should gain an
interest in the Savior's blood!
Died he for me who caused his pain? For
me who him to death pursued?
Amazing love! How can it be that thou,
my God should die for me?

He left his Father's throne above (so
free, so infinite his grace!),
Emptied himself of all but love, and
bled for Adam's helpless race.

'Tis mercy all, immense and free, for
O, My God, it found out me!

No condemnation now I dread,
Jesus, and all in him is mine;
Alive in him, my living Head, and
clothed in righteousness divine,
Bold I approach the eternal throne,
and claim the crown,
Through Christ my own.

Chapter 12

They Will Kill Him

They will condemn him … and kill him.
—Mark 10:34

ACCORDING TO MATTHEW, MARK, AND Luke, Jesus spent most of his ministry in the north part of Israel, in the towns around the Sea of Galilee, and he finished with a final journey south to Jerusalem. That journey was timed so that he could be in Jerusalem for the Passover feast, which occurs in the springtime.

Passover was one of the three festivals during which the entire population of Israel made a pilgrimage to the temple in Jerusalem. During the existence of the temple (prior to 70 CE), Passover was connected to the offering of the "first fruits" of the barley harvest, because barley was the first grain to ripen and be harvested in the land of Israel. The three festivals, now associated with the Exodus, began as agricultural and seasonal feasts but eventually became completely identified with the central theme of Israel's deliverance from oppression at the hands of God.

In the days leading up to these festivals, the highways became jammed with the faithful all moving in one direction: toward Jerusalem. Sources estimate that the population of Jerusalem during the time of Jesus was probably around eighty to one hundred thousand. But during the Passover, hundreds of thousands of Jews would pour into Jerusalem. The estimated number of people who visited Jerusalem for the Passover was around three million, both Jews and Gentiles. The historian Josephus said that there were 2.7 million people within the walls of Jerusalem when the Romans destroyed it in 70 CE. The country of Israel as a whole contained around three to four million inhabitants.

Luke tells us, "As the time approached when Jesus was to be taken up into heaven, he set his face to go to Jerusalem" (Luke 9:51). When Jesus joined the throngs headed toward Jerusalem, he knew what would happen to him there. He knew it was his time to depart this earthly life and "be taken up into heaven." But he went anyway.

As they traveled, Jesus and his friends stopped occasionally to rest and refresh in Samaria, Jericho, and other towns and villages. During these stops, Jesus often found himself in a position to pray with and heal someone. These healings did not go unnoticed by the other travelers. Many were attracted to this compassionate man and began to stay close to him so they could hear him when he talked. By the time they crested the Mount of Olives and the temple came into view, there were enough people traveling with him that it was impossible not to notice their particular group.

When the travelers saw the city, they began to cheer and dance, perhaps because they knew their long journey was over and it was all (literally) downhill from there. But when Jesus saw the city, he shed a tear, and those close to him could hear him say,

> O Jerusalem, if only you knew on this of all days the things that lead to peace. But now they are hidden from your eyes. (Luke 19:41)

It's not likely that very many in the crowd heard this lament of Jesus. They were too caught up in the excitement of the moment. Word had circulated that Jesus was going to Jerusalem to challenge the political and religious leaders with his new ideas about how people ought to be treated. When he had his disciples bring a small donkey for him to ride through the gates of the city, they remembered the words from the prophet.

> Look, your king will come to you. He is righteous and victorious. He is humble and riding on an ass, on a colt, the offspring of a donkey. (Zechariah 9:9)

They began cheering wildly. They threw garments on the road in front of him in the manner of an early red carpet. They cut long fronds off the palm trees in the area so they could be held up above the heads of the crowd and be seen from the walls of the city. People who had felt the harshness of the Roman occupiers and the restrictions of the strict legalists among the Pharisees were feeling a sense of triumph now that they had a leader who seemed poised to crush their oppressors and free them from the heel of Rome! The moment soon came to be referred to by the church as Jesus's "triumphant entry" into Jerusalem.

But there is an element to the story that makes it an even greater triumph than anyone in that throng that day could imagine. For some time, Jesus had known exactly what would happen to him in Jerusalem. He had told his disciples on more than one occasion what would happen. There was no question in his mind what would happen.

When they were in the region of Caesarea Philippi, way up in the north country, where he had asked them who they thought he was and Peter answered, "You are the Christ, the Son of God," he tried to tell them what lay ahead for him.

> Then he began to teach them that [he] must undergo great suffering, and be rejected by the elders, the chief priests, and the scribes, and be killed, and after three days rise again. (Mark 8:31)

Not long after that, when they were returning to Capernaum, their base of operations on the north shore of the Sea of Galilee, he tried again to tell them exactly what he was facing.

> From there Jesus and his followers went through Galilee, but he didn't want anyone to know it.

This was because he was teaching his disciples, "I will be delivered into human hands. They will kill me. Three days after I am killed I will rise up." But they didn't understand this kind of talk, and they were afraid to ask him. (Mark 9:30–32)

And now, on that final leg of the journey toward Jerusalem, he told them in greater detail than before what was about to happen/

> Jesus and his disciples were on the road, going up to Jerusalem, with Jesus in the lead. The disciples were amazed while the others following behind were afraid. Taking the twelve aside again, he told them what was about to happen to him. "Look!" he said. "We're going up to Jerusalem. The Son of Man will be handed over to the chief priests and the legal experts. They will condemn me to death and hand me over to the Gentiles. They will ridicule me, spit on me, torture me and kill me. After three days, I will rise up." (Mark 10:32–34)

In these months of the worldwide COVID-19 virus pandemic, much has been said about the heroic actions of those in the medical professions, law enforcement, and workers in what we now call essential occupations. We are all thankful for those who continue to go to work in and around the sick, and who deliver the vital services we need, all while knowing that they are risking their health and safety—and possibly even their lives. And indeed they deserve the label *hero* for their selfless willingness to serve others in spite of the dangerous possibilities they face. As we know, several nurses, doctors, law enforcement personnel, and others have died as a result of their sacrifices.

In *To Kill a Mockingbird*, Atticus Finch tells his son, "I wanted you to see what real courage is, instead of getting the idea that courage is a man with a gun in his hand. It's when you know you're licked before you begin but you begin anyway and you see it through no matter what. You rarely win, but sometimes you do." (To Kill A Mockingbird; by Harper Lee; Harper Perennial Modern Classics; 2002page 128) The courage being shown by these essential public servants is truly inspiring!

We might be tempted to compare the actions of today's heroes to those of Jesus as he entered Jerusalem to face down those opposed to him. But there is a difference.

For today's medical and first responder heroes, for the pharmacists, and for grocery store workers, they know there is the possibility they will contract the virus and possibly die from it. The difference is that Jesus knew that death was exactly what he was walking into. There was no question about it—arrest, humiliation, torture, and painful execution. He had known it for some time. It was not a possibility, not an option, not a percentage of a chance. That was what was going to happen. While others along that road were chanting his triumph, Jesus knew he was going to his death.

Understanding this is important because it excludes the idea that somehow Jesus was a loser! That Jesus lost. That Jesus made a bad choice by going to Jerusalem where the police were looking for him. That Jesus allowed himself to get trapped in a situation that he couldn't get out of. That he could have, should have done something else rather than walk straight into the clutches of those who were out to kill him.

Jesus's entry into Jerusalem was not a triumph because he was about to overpower his enemies. It was not a victory because he finally had a massive crowd behind him shouting his name. Jesus's deliberate, public entry into Jerusalem was more than heroic—it was salvific! Jesus entered Jerusalem and followed the path that led him to the cross, the grave, and Easter morning to prove that evil cannot silence truth, hatred cannot overpower love, and death has no power over life!

For that reason, I have chosen Mark 10:34 as the foundational text for this chapter.

> "Look!" he said, "We are going up to Jerusalem where I will be handed over to the chief priests and the legal experts. They will condemn me to death and hand me over to the Gentiles. They will ridicule me, spit on me, torture me, and kill me."

For a long time, I have debated with myself whether God knew when he sent Jesus into the world that it would end with his suffering and death on the cross. Wasn't there any other way it could have ended?

It seems to me that there was another possible outcome. It could have ended the way it was apparently intended to end: That the world might be saved through him! That his teaching would penetrate the hearts of even the most hateful and self-centered of humanity. That neighbors would accept that everyone else is their neighbor and love them, and that enemies would lay down their swords and their hatred and learn the ways that lead to peace. That the hungry would all be fed and the sick tended to. That forgiveness and compassion and sacrifice would become a way of life, and all the world would be united in peace.

That would have been another ending, right? That was the original plan after all, wasn't it? That was the goal.

But it was not going to happen that way. God knew that. We humans have a long track record of not complying with what is best for us. Jesus also knew that though there were many people believing in him and following him, most of them still had questions and doubts and confusions about his message.

He also knew that when he was no longer standing right there in front of them, cheering them on, they would lose their courage to continue to turn the world upside down. They would chicken out. They would lose interest and move on to some safer new thing. He could tell that they would soon think, like Paul would later say, "If it is for this life only that we have hoped in Christ [and tried to follow his example] then, we of all people are most to be pitied" (1 Corinthians 15:19).

Jesus knew that his message of eternal life would never be completely believed—could not be completely comprehended—unless the people had proof. Unless they could see that life continues after death. Unless they could see someone who was dead live again. And the only way for him to show us that would be for him to die and then rise up from death.

When Jesus rode into Jerusalem that day, with the crowds shouting and cheering in the background, he knew that he would be arrested, tried, and executed in a very short period of time. He knew there would be pain. He knew his friends would be devastated. But he also knew that was the only way to pull back the veil and reveal the truth about life: that life includes death, but life does not end at death.

When we celebrate Easter, we are not celebrating the time when God almost lost but in the end somehow "pulled victory out of a hat" by restoring Jesus to life. We are celebrating, once again, the complete authority that our God has over death and life.

Today, we remember the total commitment of our Lord to us shown in his willingness to "set his face toward Jerusalem" and to walk the "road of tears" to the "place of the cross" knowing the whole time that he would die there. We are humbled by his commitment to suffer death when he could have avoided Jerusalem altogether.

Yes, we praise those today who work to heal the virus-stricken, and who run into the fires, who serve in law enforcement and the military. But today's heroes all do what they do with a hope that they will survive the ordeal. Jesus entered Jerusalem with no hope of avoiding death. He entered Jerusalem knowing there would be a cross and a grave.

God loved the world so much that he sent his Son into the world. Jesus loved the world so much that he went to death on the cross to reveal total love to us.

Today's foundational text tells us that Jesus knew exactly what would happen to him in Jerusalem. It informs us that the events that led to Jesus suffering on the cross were not a series of tragic events that ultimately overpowered God's plan until Jesus was forced to suffer because there was no other option. Jesus knew exactly what would happen to him.

Jesus knew that if he avoided death at the hands of the sinful forces of this world, he would never be able to convince us that all that he had said about eternal life in the presence of the Father was true.

Jesus knew that he had come from the Father and would return to the Father.

Jesus knew that there was nothing that could separate him, or us, from the Father.

The triumph we celebrate on Palm Sunday is the triumph of love over fear and hatred, the triumph of covenant over cowardice.

I'm not sure how long it was after all these things happened that his friends remembered the time when Jesus had said to them, "If anyone would follow me, he must take up his cross and follow" (Matthew 16:24), for, "those who don't pick up their crosses and follow me aren't worthy of me" (Matthew 10:38).

But they did remember. He did say those things, and he meant for those who would follow him to have enough trust in the Father to be willing to live by Jesus's example, obeying his commandment and knowing that there is nothing they can do to us to rip us apart from the eternal love of God.

Almighty God,
You sent your Son, Jesus Christ, to save the world.
He told us of your endless love, he
showed us your love for all people.
He promised us abundant and eternal life
in the place you have prepared for us.
He suffered for us; he sacrificed for us; he
forgave us; he invited us to follow.
But only by his death on the cross are we
able to trust the truth of eternal life.
No words can ever adequately express our
gratitude for what Jesus did for us.
We pray that our lives will be the lived evidence
of the thanks that is in our hearts.
Amen.

Chapter 13

Raised from the Dead

He is not here, because he's been raised from the dead.
Matthew 28:7

HAVE YOU EVER MADE GREAT plans only to have the rug pulled out from under you? RayaSue and I wanted to really celebrate our fiftieth wedding anniversary in a big way, so we planned a great European vacation! We were going to fly to Milan, Italy, where we were going to view Michelangelo's *Last Supper*. From there we were going to take the train to Zermatt, Switzerland, to see (not climb) the Matterhorn. We were then going to train to Interlaken and Bern before training to Paris to see the Eiffel Tower, the Louvre, and (what's left of) Notre Dame. We had reservations for an anniversary dinner on a riverboat along the Seine. From there we were headed through the Chunnel to London. We were so excited! Plane tickets were purchased, hotels were booked, and I had even prepacked some essential travel items.

It turns out we spent our fiftieth anniversary quarantine at home due to the COVID-19 pandemic. Whoosh—there went the rug! Great plans. Great excitement. Great dreams. Great hopes. All gone. If you have ever felt such a great disappointment and been left wondering what to do next, then you can begin, in a small way, to relate to the emotions in the community of Jesus's followers on that Saturday after the crucifixion. They had such glorious hopes for the future under his leadership, but suddenly all their hopes and plans were crushed. All they had believed in was gone.

There are two foundational texts in this chapter. The first is from Matthew.

> After the Sabbath, at dawn on the first day of the week, Mary Magdalene and the other Mary came to look at the tomb. Look, there was a great earthquake, for an angel from the Lord came down from heaven. Coming to the stone, he rolled it away and sat on it. Now his face was like lightning and his clothes as white as snow. The guards were so terrified of him that they shook with fear and became like dead men. But the angel said to the women, "Don't be afraid. I know that you are looking for Jesus who was crucified. He isn't here, because he's been raised from the dead just as he said. Come see the place where they laid him. Now hurry, go and tell his disciples, 'He's been raised from the dead.'" (Matthew 28:1–7a)

Crucifixion was certainly not the most efficient means of execution; it required material, tools, man-hours, security guards, and time. The reason for using crucifixion was that it was a slow, painful, publicly humiliating way to put someone to death. It made a statement. Those who were crucified were generally political prisoners. It was intended to make a point to the populace not to try the patience of the government. The message was that the power of Rome was more powerful than any discontented, rebellious, revolutionary group, or ideology that may try to challenge the empire.

The public nature of death by crucifixion was intended to quell any rumors that whoever died on the cross might not have really died and could possibly be alive. It was just that kind of rumor that the chief priests and legal authorities were trying to keep from spreading by posting guards at Jesus's tomb. The rumor that they did try to spread was that his friends had come in the night and stolen the body.

But when the women and then Peter and John went to the tomb, not only did they find it open and empty, but they saw Jesus. Those were confusing encounters—thinking he was the gardener, or an angel. But it was him! Later, in the room where they were gathered, there was no confusion when he was suddenly among them, talking with them, eating with them, and letting them touch him. That was a lot to take in and sort out, but there he was, alive!

He stayed with them for many days, and hundreds of people saw him and believed it was him and that he was alive. They spread the word, and there was nothing the power of Rome could do to silence them.

They went to the cemetery to find him, but he was not there. Instead, he found them where they were gathered in their grief, and he turned that grief into joy! During the COVID-19 pandemic, we all experienced something that the world has never known: the fear of leaving our homes and being with other people, even our dying relatives. We became afraid of talking face-to-face with others because of the virus.

We have all heard now or have read the reports of the 1918 influenza pandemic with deaths of fifty to one hundred million people—one-fifth of the world's population. And as we watch the growing tallies of COVID-19 deaths every day, we wonder when it will stop, and whether we will be around when it does.

Isolation does uncomfortable things to our thoughts. Will I be forgotten? Is anybody thinking about me? Does my life have any value? Will I be missed?

The message of Easter was not just the empty tomb that morning. Before the day was out, the One whom they thought had died was standing among them. He came to them to calm their worries and fears. The Easter message is not just about Jesus rising from the dead. It is also about Jesus being with those whom he loved and bringing them the assurance that death had not taken him away from them.

The Easter message is that just because we are isolated and afraid, we are not alone. Jesus is not hindered from being with us by our closed doors. Jesus is with you, and you don't have to put on a mask to talk to him. He won't give you the virus! What he will give you is the peace of knowing that social distancing from each other does not include putting any distance between your heart and the loving heart of Jesus. He is alive and is with you wherever you are in isolation.

If you find that you have been thinking too much about your isolation and distance from your friends and, well, everyone, then my suggestion is for you to think about the One who is with you. He came to them on the day when their world was shattered, and they felt so alone that it was painful. Remember and trust that foundational text from chapter 2.

> Joseph's master took him and threw him in jail, the place where the king's prisoners were held. While he was in jail, the Lord was with Joseph and remained loyal to him. (Genesis 39:20–21)

Joseph, God's faithful one, was unjustly imprisoned; he was isolated, but God was with him. God was loyal to him. Joseph felt isolated, but he was not alone because God was with him. The message is that whether in this life or the next, whether we are socially distancing, self-isolating, or unjustly imprisoned, we are not alone. The risen Christ is with us and will be through it all. Thanks be to God!

The second foundational text is from John 11:25–26.

> Jesus said to her, "I am the resurrection and the

life. Whoever believes in me will live, even though they die. Everyone who lives and believes in me will never die."

These were the words Jesus himself spoke to the sisters of Lazarus as they grieved over his death. "Those who believe in me will live, even though they die." To really grasp Jesus's meaning, we have to rethink the way we generally think of the word *death*. Unlike the common understanding of death as the final moment of life, Jesus was saying that life includes death—not at the end of life, but somewhere very early, near the beginning.

Life includes death. Life is the constant. Death is the momentary event that separates life in one place from life in another place. Death separates life in this physical world and this physical body from life in a spiritual place and a spiritual body. What does that place look like? What will that body look like? Our minds cannot conceive, nor can our words describe, that which is beyond the physical. Because Jesus did not try to draw us a picture, we can assume that those details are not important. What Jesus said was that when life continues past the moment of death, it will be lived in the presence of the loving Father, in his house, at his feet. And Jesus will be there as well.

The message of Easter is that life includes death, but death does not end life.

From the beginning, people have always thought about and hoped for life beyond the grave. For that reason, ancient graves that archeologists have discovered have included, along with the bodies, things that their families and friends thought they would need in the life beyond the grave. Things like food, tools, money, and even boats to cross over whatever waters there might be.

We find evidence of this universal hope in the scriptures (written before Jesus's resurrection). For example,

> Even though I walk through the valley of the shadow of death, I will fear no evil, for you are with me. Your rod and your staff they protect me. You set a table for me right in front of my enemies. (Psalm 23:4–5)

Also, in the Book of Daniel we read,

> Many of those who sleep in the dusty land will wake up—some to eternal life, others to shame and eternal disgrace. Those skilled in wisdom will shine like the sky. Those who lead many to righteousness will shine like the stars forever and always. (Daniel 12:2–3)

Those hopes for a continuance of life beyond the grave were real and, perhaps, comforting. But truly no one could really rest comfortably in the hope that there is life after death without some actual evidence of it.

When Jesus rose on Easter morning and revealed himself to his disciples, those dreams became a promise, hope became faith, and fear became confidence. Easter is not just the celebration of Jesus's rising. It is also the celebration of what that moment means for us. Eternal life is promised to us. Easter is the confirmation of that promise. The message of Easter is twofold: Jesus rose, and we will rise!

Without the promise and evidence of life after death, living becomes a frustrating, useless, meaningless, and depressing event. It would be like making plans for a great trip—arranging the itinerary, deciding on all the hotels, making all the reservations, packing the suitcases, and heading off to the airport—while knowing that the trip won't happen. The flight will be cancelled, or a pandemic will force you into quarantine.

The message of resurrection is like the "Breaking News" flash that comes across the TV screen and says, "This just in! It isn't all over when you die! We've just received reports that Jesus, who was crucified, dead, and buried, has just been seen alive and is with his friends. This is apparently the same Jesus who is reported as having said, 'If you live and believe in me, you will never die. And if you die, you will still be alive!' Now, back to your regular life—but without all the dread."

Easter tells us that every day is a day to celebrate life, not to worry about death. Death is but a brief moment in a life that never ends. That is foundational!

> If we have a hope in Christ only for this life, then we deserve to be pitied more than anyone else. But in fact Christ has been raised from the dead … as in Adam all die, so in the same way all will be given everlasting life in Christ … This is what I'm saying, brothers and sisters: flesh and blood can't

go to heaven … but all of us will be changed—in an instant, in the blink of an eye, at the final trumpet. The trumpet will blast and the dead will be raised with bodies that won't decay, and we will be changed. And when this rotting body has been clothed in what can't decay, and the dying body has been clothed in what can't die, then we will know that death has been swallowed up by a victory! (1 Corinthians 15:19–28)

Life includes death, but death is not the end of life.

An Easter Prayer from the 1100s
Adam of St. Victor

I see flames of orange, yellow and red
shooting upwards to the sky,
piercing the whole clouds.
I see the clouds themselves chasing the flames upwards,
and I feel the air itself reaching for the heavens.
Down below I see great, grey rocks
beating against the earth,
as if they were pushing their way down to hell.
At your resurrection that which is light
and good rises up with you,
and that which is heavy and evil is pushed downwards.
At your resurrection goodness breaks from evil,
life breaks free from death.

Chapter 14

A Three-Ply Cord

A three-ply cord doesn't easily snap.
—Ecclesiastes 4:12

IT IS WONDERFUL TO KNOW the great stories of the Bible and to draw comfort from them. In times of personal stress or grief, to be able to read the events that surrounded the death of Lazarus and the words of Jesus to his grieving sisters can be very reassuring. When facing a daunting task for which you do not feel capable, the story of David and Goliath ought to give inspiration. And on and on. The Bible is a comfort, an encouragement, a source of strength, a guide to making decisions, and a help in all of life's trying situations.

But knowing the Bible that way is like walking into the kitchen on Thanksgiving Day right after the turkey has been taken out to the table. You see the pan with the bits and pieces that fell off bones and nibble on them because they are so good—but there's a whole turkey in the next room, and you're missing it!

With the guidance of the Holy Spirit and the inspiration and dedication of a lot of believers and prophets and disciples, the Bible that we read was written, compiled, edited, translated, and passed to us so we can know the message that God wants us to have. The Bible is some history, some poetry, some court records, some letters, some biography, and some truly bizarre visions! The Bible is not the complete history of the world. The Bible is not a scientific journal.

The Bible is the true account of a small tribe of homeless, landless wanderers living in a world where everywhere they went, they encountered other people who seemed to have different ideas and sometimes disturbing beliefs about the power that is above all powers. And they each believed that their gods, in their locations, were the best.

This small wandering tribe (who were our ancestors) started out believing that a new God had called their family to a better land. They learned that the God of Abraham and the others was with them no matter what borders they crossed. They eventually came to understand that the God whose name they did not feel privileged enough to speak (so they just wrote YHWH) was greater than, more powerful than, and more knowing than all the other ideas of gods people believed in. They eventually came to express not just that their God was the greatest of all the gods but that there is only one God, with no name to describe his power and authority because any earthly name would be limiting. The God of our people is simply the great "I Am."

As they wandered and learned more about their God, they had all sorts of encounters with friendly and hostile neighbors (mostly hostile), and they passed those stories on to their children. The stories are fun and exciting and enlightening, but by themselves they don't tell the best part of the story. They are the crumbs in the turkey pan. But what is the relationship that God wants to have with us? What is God prepared to give to us or do for us, and what does God expect from us in return? What is the foundation upon which that relationship is built?

Jesus told the story (in Matthew 7:24ff) about the two houses that were built by two well-intentioned men. The first fellow had an elaborate set of plans drawn up for his lavish home. He wanted the best fixtures and appliances and landscaping. He had such expensive dreams that when he sat down to add up the costs, he realized that his bank account was a little light! Not wanting to give up any of the fine things he had hoped for, he told the builder to cut back on the foundation; no one would ever see that anyway.

The other man had dreams just as fine as his neighbor, but he knew that the foundation upon which his house would be built was the most important part of it. He made sure his builders kept digging deeper and deeper until they hit solid rock. Then he laid his foundation and his house stood long past when he could remember what that other guy's mansion had looked like before the great storm washed it away.

The Bible contains sixty-six different books, but it is one book. There are over thirty thousand verses in the Bible, but there is just one theme. The Bible was written over a thousand-year span of time, but it centers around one message. The Bible talks about people of many cultures, many languages, many political persuasions, and many faith traditions, but its message is universal.

I have written each chapter in this little book around one or two verses that I think are so critically important to the Bible story that they are foundational to the whole Bible. For the most part, these verses are repeated throughout the Bible, sometimes with exactly the same words, but often with slight variations depending on the moment and context. I believe that when these verses are braided together like the three-ply cord that is mentioned in Ecclesiastes 6:9, they will provide a strong foundation upon which a personal faith can be built with no threat of being washed away by storms of question and doubt.

Supremely good

It began with the creation. God gave his approval at each step in the process, but when it was all finished, God took a step back and looked over it all and pronounced, "It is supremely good!" All of the creation is good! It is a dynamic system, which means it has moving parts, but each part is good: hurricanes, earthquakes, tornados—all of it! It is growing, it is changing, it is shifting, and it is becoming. And it seems the whole thing was created so that we could have life in extravagant abundance: things to eat, things to smell, places to go, and people to meet. This place is great! If the creation was not completely or supremely good, that would put us in the position of living with unrelenting uncertainty. Living in a creation in which some parts are not good would be like living in a mine field where every move could be fatal. But this creation is supremely good.

Emmanuel (God is with us)

The creation is also very complex and difficult to navigate, which is why it is also foundational to know that the Creator, God, is here with us. God watches us like any excited parent watches over a child: to see how we react when discovering new things, to guide us in safer and healthier directions than we might otherwise go. God is with us because God doesn't want us to be afraid; remember, that's what the angels said every time they appeared, "Do not be afraid." God has a hope for each one of us: that we may discover beauty and joy and live in the warmth of love all our days and in all our relationships.

All things

Believing that the creation is supremely good, and that God is with us every step we take, it follows that whatever happens in this life has the potential to be good. As Joseph said to his brothers, "Even though you intended to do harm to me, God intended it for good." We have to believe that we are not smart enough, mean enough, selfish enough, or evil enough to be able to turn God's good plan into something bad. In all things that happen, there is the potential for something good to be the result.

Even though everything God created is good, not everything that results from human action or interaction with each other is good. But by following God's will for our living, which includes loving, forgiving, serving, and sacrificing, goodness will grow out of the devastation of badness.

I hear you

Because God is with us, we can trust that God "sees the misery of his people. God hears our cries on account of our oppressors. God knows our sufferings, and God has come to deliver us." If I were to suggest a center point for the foundation, it would be this one from Exodus 3:7 and its New Testament parallel in John 3:16. God loves the world so completely that he came into the world in our own form so that we could see God and know exactly what God's plan for us is, and so that we might fully enjoy the gift God has given us in the creation and in the life beyond this life.

When God expelled the man and woman from paradise (for our own good, so that we would not eat any more of the forbidden fruits), God was with them on the outside of the gate, not locked away from them in the garden. The rest of the Bible from that moment is the record of God's continuous presence with his people—whether we recognized it or not.

If my people

Everywhere the Hebrew people went, they encountered folk who believed in some system of sacrificial offering to get the attention and blessing of their gods. They thought their gods wanted to be fed (I suppose "a well-fed god is a happy god" is what they believed). So they burned portions of their crops and killed the best of their animals (and at times their children) to please their gods. The Hebrews adopted these practices at first. But eventually they began to hear God telling them that was not what he wanted. "The sacrifice acceptable to God is a broken spirit and contrite heart" (Psalm 51:17).

What God wants from us is to humble ourselves, to step out from behind our arrogance so we can see the power of God at work, to pray, to listen for the voice of God guiding us, to turn from our wicked ways—and we know what those ways are. They are the ways that separate us from each other and destroy what love builds. They are the ways of greed, hatred, fear, and injustice. When God says, "If my people will humble themselves, pray, and turn from their wicked ways—then will I heal their land," that sounds like a foundational statement to understand what God wants from us in this relationship (and a good suggestion to address what ails our land).

My shepherd

How does God relate to us? Is God a ruthless taskmaster, punishing us for every mistake we make? Is God a cruel tyrant, always demanding and never giving? Is God a capricious master, always changing his mind and never predictable? Whatever God is like is foundational to our relationship with God.

"The Lord is my shepherd." The Lord knows my needs, my weaknesses, my inabilities, and my fears. The Lord is the good shepherd who leads me to grassy resting places; to fresh, still waters; and along the paths that will bring me goodness. The Lord is with me in the darkest of days and when I am surrounded by enemies. The Lord feeds me, fills me, and invites me into his eternal house. That's how God is to us.

What God wants

What is it that God wants from me in return for all his blessings? What are the stipulations of the contract that I am agreeing to when I sign on to be one of Christ's children? What is the long list of things that I will have to do?

Here's the list: Do justice. Love kindness. Walk humbly. Love God. Love one another. That's it. "Do this and you shall live" (Luke 10:28). Don't try to make it more difficult than that—not that it's always easy to do those things. Let everything you do build from this foundation. It's all about how we treat others, how we respect them, how we serve them, how we forgive and encourage them and how we love them. These things are foundational.

Every sin

But what if I mess up? How many times can I sin before I am off God's nice list? What are the things I can do that are a line too far?

The truth, from the mouth of Jesus, is there is nothing you can do that is not forgivable by God (Mark 3:28). There is no sin that is too extreme that makes it unforgivable. There is no limit to the number of times that your sins will be forgiven. Well, except one. Let me explain.

You have to understand that God doesn't forgive sins on a case-by-case basis. God doesn't sit around his office every day going over the long lists of all our sins and deciding which ones merit forgiveness and which ones don't. The way God has decided to handle the issue of our sins (all of them) is to nail them to the cross and forgive all of them through the death of Jesus. Jesus died for the forgiveness of the sins of the whole world. Through his suffering, Jesus paid the price for our sin. This is a gift offered to each of us—blanket, unlimited forgiveness.

The only thing that could prevent your sins from being included in this offer would be for you to reject the gift. For you to say (with the way you live), "No, thank you. I don't believe in you. I don't think you have anything I want. I reject your offer." (In the olden days, they called that blasphemy. I call it stupidity.)

When you pray

What is the best way to address this God who created the entire universe, who looks over us, who walks with us, and who forgives all our sinfulness? What is the proper title? Almighty God? All-Knowing Ruler of All? King of the Universe? Lord of Lords? King of Kings? Those are all wonderful and appropriate titles for God, but they are a bit unnecessary. On addition to all those images, God is a loving parent. God is a nurturing mother. God is a concerned father.

When his friends asked Jesus to teach them how to pray, he began by telling them that they could simply refer to God as Father. (I'm betting that he would approve of Mother as well.) Unless we can relate to God in such an intimate way, we will always be a little cautious when talking to him. To be given permission to call God "our Father" is foundational for a close, personal relationship with God.

A great paradox

One foundational principle that sets the followers of Jesus apart from everyone else is the great paradox that we should love our enemies as well as our friends and neighbors. The reason this is necessary is that love is a perfect thing. When we say, "God is love," we mean that God is only love. God is always love. God is perfect love. When God loves, God loves 100 percent—never to any lesser degrees.

If we are to "love one another the way God loves us," then we are to love completely, without judgment or distinction. We are to strive to be made perfect in the way we love. We are to love the way Jesus loved. And we cannot say we love the way Jesus loved us and not include our enemies in that love we have for others.

God so loved the world

In chapter 4, I talked about John 3:16 as a foundational text. I believe it is so for two reasons. First, as I said, it is in fulfillment of the promise that God wanted to be with us and for us to know it. God sent the Christ into the world because God loves us enough to be with us and suffer on our behalf. The second reason this passage is so fundamental to the whole biblical message is that God wanted all of humanity to be saved from separation from God. The purpose for which God "gave his only begotten Son" was so that no one who believes in him will perish but will have eternal life.

The Christ did not to come into the world to judge the world. If that were the case, we would all be condemned, doomed with no expectation of leniency. The Christ, in the person of Jesus, was sent into the world for the purpose and possibility of saving the world from the destructive consequences of our own sinfulness. The incarnation of God's love in human form happened to give us a way out of the chaos we are so adept at creating. Sending Jesus is proof of the extent God is willing to go to love us—before we even thought about loving God.

They will kill him

Fundamental to the Christian worship of the Christ is a firm belief that Jesus knew that in Jerusalem, they would kill him. His arrest, trial, suffering, crucifixion, and death on the cross did not happen because he could not find a way to escape. Jesus was not a loser in the struggle to show which was stronger, Rome or God. Jesus knew that the goodness that he represented would elicit the most violent reaction from the powers of the world. He knew that encounter between holiness and sinfulness would result in his death.

But Jesus also knew that there is life beyond death, and the only way to prove that to our limited, finite minds was to actually show us. Jesus died on the cross so that he could rise from the grave. Jesus told this to his disciples in Mark 10:34. They were confused about it when he said it, and they tried to tell him to stop talking about it. But later, when they were trying to make sense of what seemed like the ultimate defeat, they remembered that he had said those things. And having said them, they knew that his death on the cross was a victory, not defeat.

Raised from the dead

Not only was the stone rolled away and the tomb empty, but he met them there and talked to them. He was among them at the table, and he ate with them. He followed them to the boat and watched them through the night, and in the morning he cooked breakfast for them. He walked with them, talked to them, and invited them to continue to follow him—with no sign of anger or retaliation for their having denied him.

Once again, it is fundamental to read that God was with them. That God was reaching out to them, that God had work for them to do, that God loved them (and us). That not even the worst they (and we) could do to him could get him to stop loving us.

In the thirty thousand verses in the Bible, there are many that are intimidating for someone trying to read the Bible for the first time. There are many that seem to paint a very dark picture of a warlike, vengeful God. There are others that are not very helpful at all unless you are really into ancient Hebrew genealogy. There are some that are confusing because they seem to contradict others. But I still maintain that there is one positive, hopeful, consistent message throughout the Bible, from Genesis to Revelation. And that message is that the God who created us loves us, is with us, wants us to have a great experience while we are living this life, and wants us to return home to his house, where we will live in his presence for eternity.

There are certainly other texts that can be counted as foundational to this message. I hope when you find one, you will underline it, put a star in the margin next to it, and rejoice and be glad in it!

Index of Scripture References

Chapter 1

Genesis 1:31
Mark 10:17–18
Psalm 8

Chapter 2

Genesis 39:21
Exodus 3:11–12
Deuteronomy 31:6
Joshua 1:9
Matthew 1:23
Matthew 28:20
Romans 8:38
Romans 10:13–14

Chapter 3

Genesis 50:20
Genesis 50:17–18
Genesis 41:51–52
Romans 8:28
Romans 8:31, 35, 37–39

Chapter 4

Exodus 2:23–25
Exodus 32:7–10
Joshua 1:1
Judges 2:18
Isaiah 61:1–2a
John 3:16

Chapter 5

2 Chronicles 7:14
2 Chronicles 3–4
2 Chronicles 5:12–13
2 Chronicles 7:10–14
Hosea 6:6
Micah 6:8
Isaiah 1:11–17
James 1:27

Chapter 6

Psalm 23
1 Samuel 17:34–37

John 10:11–16
Psalm 100:3
Daniel 12:2
Psalm 25

Chapter 7

Micah 6:8
Exodus 23:6
Deuteronomy 24:17
Isaiah 1:17; 61:8
Jeremiah 21:12; 22:3
Hosea 12:6
Amos 5 24
Matthew 12:6; 22:35–40
John 15:12
Proverbs 21:3

Chapter 8

Romans 3:22
Exodus 29:13–14
Numbers 5:6–7
Matthew 1:21; 6:14–15
Matthew 18:21; 16:28
Mark 3:28–29
Genesis 9:14–15
Micah 7:18–19
1 John 2:1–2; 4:10
Jeremiah 31:2
Psalm 136
Mark 3:28–29
1 John 1:9
Proverbs 28:13
Colossians 1:9–14

Chapter 9

Matthew 6:5–8; 9–14
1 Chronicles 29:11–13

Chapter 10

Matthew 23:11
Mark 9:35
2 Corinthians 12:10
Romans 12:2
Romans 8:31–39
Philippians 2:5–11
Matthew 5:43–44
Leviticus 19:15–18
Luke 9:41–44
John 14:27
Romans 12:9–21

Chapter 11

John 3:14–18
Numbers 21:9
Matthew 5:45
Psalm 49:5–9
John 14:6–9
John 1:1–4
John 10:16

Chapter 12

Mark 10:34
Luke 9:41; 51
Zechariah 9:9
Mark 8:31
Mark 9:30–32

1 Corinthians 15:19
Matthew 10:38; 16:24

Chapter 13

Matthew 28:1–7a
Genesis 39:20–21
John 11:25–26
Psalm 23:4–5
Daniel 12:2–3
1 Corinthians 15:19–28

Chapter 14

Psalm 89:4
Matthew 7:24ff
Ecclesiastes 6:9
Exodus 3:7
John 3:16
Psalm 51:17
Luke 10:28

About the Author

Doug Hallman, DMin, is an ordained elder in the Florida Conference of the United Methodist Church. Dr. Hallman has served numerous churches in Florida and has been a college chaplain and teacher at Florida Southern College in Lakeland. Rev. Hallman, along with his wife, RayaSue, have also served as missionaries through the United Methodist General Board of Global Ministries in Venezuela and Jamaica. The Hallmans are retired and living in Lakeland, Florida

Printed in the United States
by Baker & Taylor Publisher Services